Steck-Vaughn

Reading Comprehension

Building Vocabulary and Meaning

LEVEL

Reviewers

Lee Waggener
Second Grade Teacher
Bon View Elementary
Ontario-Montclair School District
Ontario, California

Argen Hurley
First Grade Teacher
Ballast Point Elementary
Hillsborough County School District
Tampa, Florida

STECK-VAUGHN
ELEMENTARY · SECONDARY · ADULT · LIBRARY

A Harcourt Company

www.steck-vaughn.com

ACKNOWLEDGMENTS

Editorial Director Stephanie Muller

Editor Kathleen Wiseman

Assistant Editor Julie M. Smith

Associate Director of Design Cynthia Ellis

Designer Alexandra Corona

Editorial Development Jump Start Press

Design and Production MKR Design, Inc.

Senior Technical Advisor Alan Klemp

Production Coordinator Susan Tyson Fogarasi

Illustration Credits: Joy Allen: pp.86, 87, 88, 89, 90, 91, 92, 93; Lori Anzalone: pp.6; Sue Carlson: pp.3; Bob Doucet: pp.95; Meredith Johnson: pp.42, 43, 44, 45, 47, 49; Deborah Melmone: pp.10, 11, 12, 13, 14, 17; Patrick Merrell: pp.104; Alan Reingold: pp.62, 63, 64, 65, 66, 67, 68; Stacey Schuett: pp.50; Ken Spengler: pp.26, 27, 28, 29, 30, 31, 33; Elizabeth Wolf: pp.57.

Photo Credits: Cover ©Stuart Westmorland/Getty Images; p.2a ©Amos Machoum/CORBIS; p.2b ©Georgette Douwma/Getty Images; p.2c ©Chris Simpson/Getty Images; p.2d ©Georgette Douwma/Getty Images; p.2e ©Stuart Westmorland/Getty Images; p.3a ©Lawson Wood/CORBIS; p.3b ©Stuart Westmorland/Getty Images; p.4a ©David Fleetham/Getty Images; p.5a ©Chris Simpson/Getty Images; p.5b ©David Fleetham/Getty Images; p.6a ©GeorgetteDouwma/Getty Images; p.6b ©Stuart Westmorland/Getty Images; pp.8, 9a,b,c ©Chris Simpson/Getty Images; p.18b ©Tony Freeman/PhotoEdit; p.19 ©Tony Anderson/Getty Images; p.23 ©RichardCummins/CORBIS; pp.34,35,37b ©DK Images; pp.38.39,40a ©David A. Northcott/CORBIS; p.40b ©DK Images; p.41 ©Michael & Patricia Fogoen/CORBIS; p.52 ©Joe McDonald/CORBIS; p.54b ©Pablo Corral Vega/CORBIS; p.54c ©Luiz C. Marigo/Peter Arnold, Inc.; p.55 ©Mark Moffett/Minden Pictures; p.56b ©Buddy Mays/CORBIS; p.57 ©Chris Hellier/CORBIS; p.59a ©Joseph Van Os/Getty Images; p.59b ©Wolfgang Kaehler/CORBIS; p.61 ©Kevin Schafer/Getty Images; p.70 ©Anne-Marie Webber/Getty Images; p.71a ©Richard Mackson/TimePix; p.71b © Anne- Marie Webber/Getty Images; p.72a,b ©Tony Donaldson Icon SMI; p.73 ©Chris Trotman/CORBIS; p.74 ©Tony Donaldson Icon SMI; p.75 ©David Madison/Getty Images; p.76 ©Timothy A. Clary/CORBIS; p.77 ©Tony Donaldson Icon SMI; p.78a ©Hulton Archive/Getty Images; p.78b ©Gary Buss/Getty Images; p.79b ©CORBIS; p.80a ©Araldo De Luca/CORBIS; p.80b ©Hulton Archive/Getty Images; p.80e ©Tom & Dee Ann McCarthy/CORBIS; p.81a ©Colin Garratt/CORBIS; p.81b ©Hulton-Deutsch Collection/CORBIS; p.81c ©Underwood & Underwood/CORBIS; p.81d ©Hulton Archive/Getty Images; p.81f ©Angelo Hornak/CORBIS; p.81g ©AFP/CORBIS; p.81h ©Art on File/CORBIS; p.81I ©First Light/CORBIS; p.82c ©J.W. Burkey/Getty Images; p.83 ©Dave Nagel/Getty Images; p.85a ©CORBIS; p.94a ©Layne Kennedy/CORBIS; p.94b ©Superstock; p.96 ©Steve Kaufman/ CORBIS; p.97a ©L. Clarke/CORBIS; p.97b ©Eric Meola/Getty Images; p.98 ©Kevin R. Morris/CORBIS; p.101 ©Martyn Goddard/Getty Images; p.102 ©Tui De Roy/Minden Pictures; p.103 ©Mark Jones/Minden Pictures; p.106 ©Tony Freeman/PhotoEdit; p.107 ©Superstock; p.108 ©CORBIS.

Additional photography by Getty Royalty Free, Michael Groen Photography, Bob Rowan/Progressive Images.

ISBN 0-7398-5822-X

Contents

At Home in a Coral Reef

Get Ready to Read

The **main idea** of an article is what it is about. The **supporting details** are small pieces of information that tell more about the main idea. As you read about a coral reef, look for the main idea of the article and the supporting details.

Corals are animals. They live in warm, shallow seas. Corals live together in **colonies**. Colonies are colorful and form interesting shapes.

When corals die, their skeletons remain. The skeletons form layers of coral rock. Living corals grow and build on this rock. Over many years, the layers of coral rock form a **reef**. A coral reef makes up an **ecosystem**, so it is home to many plants and animals.

Life in a Reef

Many different kinds of animals live in coral reefs. Worms and crabs live in coral rock. They are **inactive** during the day. They dig holes in the rock and hide. The holes protect them from fish that eat them. When the fish are asleep at night, the worms and crabs come out to look for food.

Parrotfish live in the branches of coral. They eat **algae**. Algae grows on coral like moss grows on rocks. Algae can be harmful. It keeps the coral from growing. The parrotfish help the reef stay healthy by eating algae.

dugong

Dugongs (doo GONGZ) are sea mammals that live near the reef. They eat seaweed. This keeps seaweed from spreading. Too much seaweed can harm a reef.

The world's largest coral reef is near Australia.

N
W E
S

CORAL SEA

GREAT BARRIER REEF

AUSTRALIA

area enlarged

AUSTRALIA

★ **Tip**
The **heading** often states the main idea of a paragraph. As you read, look for details that tell about the main idea.

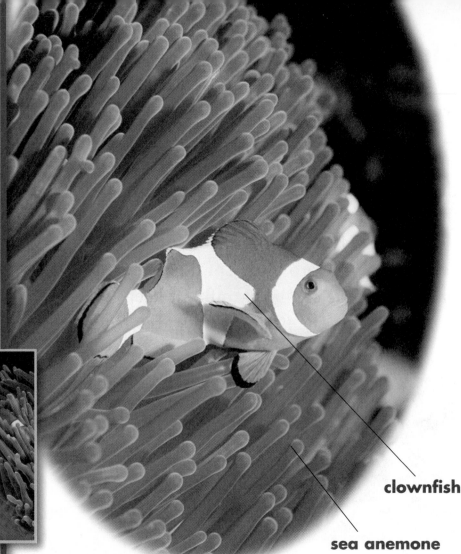

clownfish

sea anemone

VOCABULARY

tentacles
(TEN tuh kuhlz)
Long, thin parts of an animal's body used for moving or feeling

relationship
(ree LAY shuhn ship)
The way animals or things get along together

Animals Help Each Other

Some animals help each other in a reef. A sea anemone (uh NEM uh nee) looks like a plant. But it is really an animal. The sea anemone sticks to coral. It does not move. It uses its **tentacles** to sting fish. Then it eats the fish.

Clownfish often live with sea anemones. The two animals have a special **relationship**. The sea anemone protects the clownfish. It stings other fish that might eat the clownfish. It also uses its tentacles to clean the clownfish. The clownfish helps the sea anemone by attracting fish for the anemone. It does this by dropping food while it eats. When other fish come by to pick up the scraps, the sea anemone strikes!

Reefs in Danger

There are several things that **endanger** reefs. Some starfish eat coral. Large groups of starfish may eat coral faster than it can grow. This damages the reef. It can take many years for a reef to build itself again.

People also endanger reefs. They throw away harmful chemicals that wash into the sea. In some places, people catch too many fish. This upsets the balance of a reef ecosystem.

The reef is a special ecosystem for many plants and animals. Each one has a role in keeping the reef healthy. It is important to protect coral reefs and keep them safe.

coral reef

VOCABULARY

endanger
(in DAYN juhr) To cause danger

Comprehension Check

Circle the letter next to the best answer.

1. What are corals?

   A. Plants
   B. Animals
   C. Body parts
   D. Ecosystems

2. How are crabs and worms alike?

   E. They eat coral.
   F. They come out during the day to look for food.
   G. They use the coral for shelter.
   H. They eat algae.

3. What might happen if there were no more parrotfish?

   A. There would be more starfish.
   B. The dugongs would eat more algae.
   C. Coral would grow faster.
   D. Algae could cover the coral.

4. What is this article mainly about?

   E. How corals build a reef
   F. How animals harm the reef
   G. How animals and plants live together in a reef
   H. Why plants are important to a reef

Answer the questions below in complete sentences.

5. Why does a clownfish live with a sea anemone?

   _____

   _____

6. Why do you think it is important to protect coral reefs and keep them safe?

   _____

   _____

Vocabulary Builder

▶ **Write a word from the box that matches each clue. Then read the word formed by the boxed letters.**

1. Long, thin parts of an animal's body used for moving or feeling __ __ __ __ __ [1] __ __ __

2. The way animals or things get along together __ __ __ __ __ __ [2] __ __ __ __ __

3. A strip of rock, sand, or coral close to the surface of a body of water [3] __ __ __

4. Water plants __ __ __ [4] __

5. Groups that live together __ __ [5] __ __ __ __

6. A group of plants and animals that need each other to live __ __ __ [6] __ __ __ __ __

__ __ __ __ __ __
1 2 3 4 5 6

EXTEND YOUR VOCABULARY

Prefixes A prefix is a word part that is added to the beginning of a word. A prefix changes the meaning of a word.

▶ **Draw a circle around each word with a prefix. Write the meaning of the word on the line.**

en = to cause
in = not

7. Both chemicals and hungry starfish can endanger a reef.

_____

8. Corals look inactive because they grow so slowly.

_____

Main Idea and Supporting Details

The **main idea** is what an article is about. The **supporting details** tell more about the main idea.

▶ **Use the article and the main idea chart to write your answers.**

Main Idea

Many different plants and animals live together in a coral reef.

Supporting Detail

_____

_____

Supporting Detail

_____

_____

Supporting Detail

_____

_____

▶ **Answer the questions below in complete sentences.**

1. What might be another good title for this article?

_____

2. Why do worms hide in holes during the day?

_____

_____

Your Turn to Write

▷ **Choose an animal that you think is interesting. Think about where it lives, what it looks like, and how it acts. Then complete the main idea chart below.**

Main Idea

A _____ is an interesting animal.

Supporting Detail

_____

_____

Supporting Detail

_____

_____

Supporting Detail

_____

_____

▷ **On a separate sheet of paper, write a paragraph about your animal. Use your chart to help you write the paragraph.**

It's Not Easy Being Me!

What Do You Already Know?

Think about stories you know that have a wolf in them. What is the wolf like?

⭐ Get Ready to Read

A **plot** is the important events that happen in the **beginning**, **middle**, and **end** of a story. As you read the story, look for the important events that happen to Wolf as he tries to clear his name.

Dear Mom,

It's not easy being me! My reputation as the Big Bad Wolf is all wrong. I'm going to visit the Three Little Pigs and Red Riding Hood to clear my name.

Love,
Big Bob Wolf

Mother Gray Wolf
123 Pack Street
Howltown,
South Woods
22053

VOCABULARY

reputation
(REP yoo TAY shuhn)
The way people see and think about someone

cruel (KROO uhl) Mean

misunderstanding
(MIS un duhr STAN ding)
A failure to understand

nce upon a time, there was an unhappy wolf. He was tired of his lonely life and decided to set things straight.

"The Three Little Pigs must hear my side of the story," said Wolf. "They've been saying **cruel** things about me for years. But it's all a **misunderstanding**. I only want to be friends with them."

Wolf decided to visit the pigs' little brick house. He knocked on the door. One pig peeked out and shouted, "The wolf is back! By the hairs on my chinny, chin, chin, the Big Bad Wolf is back!"

"No! You have it all wrong!" Wolf called out. "My real name is Big Bob Wolf. Ever since you pigs started singing that silly song about a big bad wolf, my reputation has been ruined. I was only trying to help you."

Three pairs of eyes looked at him. "We're listening," they squealed.

"I was worried when two of you made straw and stick houses," continued Wolf. "A strong wind could have blown them down. I huffed and puffed to show you how fragile the houses were. You might have been hurt if I hadn't helped!"

"Okay, I see what you mean," answered the pig who had built the straw house.

"Good!" exclaimed Wolf. "Just come on out so that I can have you for lunch. . . ."

"See, he hasn't changed at all! Run! Hide!" squealed the pigs.

"I was going to say that I can have you *over* for lunch at my house. Anyway, I don't eat other animals," cried Wolf. "I like vegetables and noodles, not pigs and poodles!"

But it was no use. The pigs had made up their minds about Wolf.

VOCABULARY

ruined (ROO ind)
Harmed or damaged

fragile (FRAJ uhl)
Easy to break

Dear Mom,

I didn't resolve the problem with the Three Little Pigs. I'm afraid they'll always think of me as the Big Bad Wolf. I hope Red Riding Hood will listen to me.

Love,
B.B. Wolf

Mother Gray Wolf
123 Pack Street
Howltown,
South Woods
22053

★ Tip

In the **middle** of a plot, the main character tries to solve a problem. Look for how Wolf tries to solve his problem.

VOCABULARY

resolve (ri ZOLV)
To settle or solve

rumor (ROO muhr)
A story that has not been proven true

manners (MAN uhrz)
Polite ways to act

After his trouble with the little pigs, Wolf set out through the forest to find Red Riding Hood. When he arrived at her house, Wolf knocked on the door.

"Red, it's B.B. Wolf!" he called. "I want to talk about this **rumor** you've been spreading. How could you think I would hurt a sweet old lady? Please listen to my side of the story!"

Red opened the door. "I'm listening," she said.

"I knew Grandma was sick, so I brought her some soup," explained Wolf. "Then she went to the doctor. I promised to take care of you until she came back."

"Hmm. Then why were you in Grandma's bed?" asked Red.

"I was keeping it warm," answered Wolf. "Then you started to make fun of me. Hasn't Grandma taught you better **manners**? I can't help it that I have a big nose."

Then Wolf said, "By the way, I didn't say anything about eating you. I told you that my teeth were all the better to *greet* you with."

"Maybe I did misunderstand," said Red.

"You sure did!" said Wolf. "I'm willing to forget about it, though. I will even bite you for lunch."

"You're still the Big Bad Wolf!" yelled Red. She slammed the door right on his big nose.

"Wait!" cried Wolf. "I meant to say that I will *invite* you for lunch!"

In the end, Wolf did live happily ever after. He decided that he was trying to make friends with the wrong characters. Finally, Wolf found some friends who accepted him for who he was. In fact, he had a party for his new friends. The guests were Fox, Goldilocks, and a wonderful little troll who lived under a bridge.

Dear Mom,

My visit with Red Riding Hood didn't go well. Maybe I need to find some different friends. It's not easy being me!

Love,
B.B. Wolf

Mother Gray Wolf
123 Pack Street
Howltown,
South Woods
22053

Tip

Think about how Wolf solves his problem at the **end** of this story.

The End

✓ Comprehension Check

▶ Answer the questions below in complete sentences.

1. What problem does Wolf try to solve?

The problem WOlF try to solve is to clear his Name.

2. What does Wolf do about his problem?

The WOlF try to tell the Three tittle pigs that he wasn't try to blow down the houses.

3. Who does Wolf visit first?

The WOlF visit the Three little pigs First.

4. What reason does Wolf give for blowing down the pigs' houses?

5. Why didn't anyone believe Wolf when he tried to explain his actions?

6. How is the wolf in this story different from the wolf in other well-known stories?

The

Vocabulary Builder

▶ **Read the paragraph. Fill in the circle next to the word that completes each sentence.**

Everybody liked Red Riding Hood. She had a _____
1
for being kind and caring. She was always nice and polite and had

good _____. When she found out that Goldilocks broke
2
into the Bears' house, she wanted to _____ the problem.
3
As it turned out, it was all a big _____. Baby Bear had
4
actually invited Goldilocks over, but then he forgot!

1.
○ story
○ reputation
○ party
○ feeling

2.
○ manners
○ bicycle
○ smile
○ books

3.
○ excite
○ argue
○ leave
○ resolve

4.
○ surprise
○ friendship
○ happiness
○ misunderstanding

EXTEND YOUR VOCABULARY

Antonyms Antonyms are words that have opposite meanings.

▶ **Match each word in the box with its antonym.
Write each word on the correct line.**

cruel	fragile	ruined	rumor

5. kind _____

6. repaired _____

7. truth _____

8. strong _____

Plot

A **plot** is the important events in a story. All plots have a **beginning**, a **middle**, and an **end**.

▶ **Use events from the story to complete the plot chart.**

Beginning

Wolf has a bad reputation. He wants to clear his name.

▼

Middle

_____

_____

▼

End

_____

_____

▶ **Use the story and your plot chart to write the answers.**

1. Why does Wolf visit the Three Little Pigs?

_____

_____

2. Does Wolf solve his problem? Explain.

_____

_____

_____

Your Turn to Write

▷ Think about another fairy tale. What would the story be like if the bad character gave his or her point of view? Use the plot chart to plan some different story events.

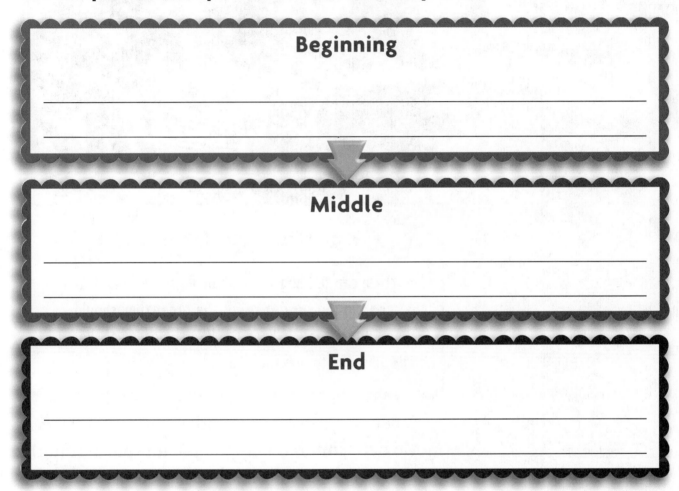

Beginning

_____

_____

Middle

_____

_____

End

_____

_____

▷ On a separate sheet of paper, rewrite the fairy tale from a different point of view. Use the information from your plot chart.

? What Do You Already Know?

Have you ever played the piñata game? What did the piñata look like? What was inside it?

fiesta (fee ES tuh)
A kind of party

traditional
(truh DISH uh nuhl)
Something that is passed down from parents to children

LET'S MAKE A PIÑATA!

⭐ Get Ready to Read

An article can tell how to make or do something. It tells the **steps** in the **sequence**, or the order they should happen. In this article keep track of the order of the steps you take to make a piñata.

Whenever there is a birthday party or a **fiesta** in Mexico, children play the piñata (pin YAH tuh) game. A piñata is a brightly decorated box. Many piñatas look like animals. The **traditional** piñata looks like a star. Candy, fruit, and small toys are hidden inside the piñata.

A piñata is hung up on a rope above children's heads. Then children take turns trying to break open the piñata with a long stick. But there's a catch. Players have to wear a blindfold when it's their turn! When the piñata finally cracks open, children race to pick up the treats that fall out.

Before You Begin

Making a piñata is fun and easy. First choose a place to work that can get dirty. The work area should be a place where the piñata can be left out safely for several days. Cover your work area with newspaper. Then gather your materials. It's time to make a piñata!

Tip

Look for time order words such as **first**, **second**, **next**, **then**, and **last** to give you clues about the order of the **steps**.

What You Will Need

- a large balloon
- 18-inch string
- 2 cups flour (473 milliliters)
- 4 cups water (946 milliliters)
- large bowl
- spoon
- about 50 strips of newspaper, 2 inches wide
- wrapped candy and small toys
- tape
- about 10 pieces of thin cardboard
- scissors
- glue
- tissue paper
- markers
- small hook

Step 1

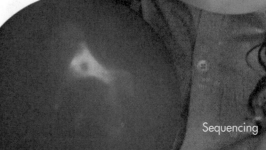

What You Will Do

Step 1 First, make the piñata frame. Blow up the balloon. Tie a knot at the end of it. Then tie the string around the knot. Now hang the balloon by its string.

mixture (MIKS chuhr)
Something made when things are stirred together

overlap (OH vuhr LAP)
To lay two things together so that they partly cover each other

Step 2

Second, form the piñata shell. Mix two cups (473 milliliters) of flour with four cups (946 milliliters) of water in a bowl. This **mixture** makes a paste that is almost as thick as glue. Dip the newspaper strips in the paste and spread them on the balloon one at a time. **Overlap** the wet strips so that the balloon is fully covered. Let the balloon dry overnight. Repeat this step twice the next day. There should be a total of three layers of newspaper strips on the balloon.

Step 2

Step 3

Step 3

Next, fill the piñata with treats. Cut a three-inch hole in the top of the piñata. Ask an adult to help. Pop the balloon and pull it out. Fill the piñata with candy and toys. The treats must be small so they will not hurt anyone when they fall out of the piñata. Then tape the hole shut.

Step 4

Then shape the piñata. Use your imagination to **design** the piñata. Draw and cut out animal **features**, such as beaks or tails, from the cardboard. You can also make the points on a star by rolling the cardboard into cone shapes. Tape the cardboard pieces on the piñata shell. You may wish to add more newspaper and paste to hold the cardboard in place.

Step 5

Last, decorate the piñata. Use brightly colored tissue paper to decorate the piñata. Cut the paper into strips. Then cut the strips to look like **fringe**. Glue the strips in rows on the piñata. You may wish to cut some more tissue paper into long paper **streamers**. Glue them on the piñata. Finally add the hook to the top of the piñata. Now you are ready to have your own fiesta!

Step 5

Comprehension Check

▶ Fill in the circle next to the best answer.

1. Where would you most likely play the piñata game?

Ⓐ In a store
Ⓑ At a party
Ⓒ At a soccer game
Ⓓ In the library

2. What do you do after you dip the newspaper strips in the paste?

Ⓔ Cut the strips to look like fringe.
Ⓕ Spread the strips on a balloon.
Ⓖ Cut a hole in the piñata.
Ⓗ Soak the strips.

3. Which of these would be put inside a piñata?

Ⓐ Tissue paper
Ⓑ A football
Ⓒ Box of raisins
Ⓓ Glue

4. Many piñatas look like —

Ⓔ cars
Ⓕ candy
Ⓖ cones
Ⓗ animals

▶ Answer the questions below in complete sentences.

5. Why should the piñata work area be covered with newspaper?

_____

_____

6. What might happen if a piñata is made with only one layer of newspaper and paste?

_____

_____

Vocabulary Builder

▶ **Write the word from the box that completes each sentence.**

design	fiesta	mixture	streamers	traditional

1. Mr. Ruiz is planning a _____ to celebrate his son's birthday.

2. He will serve some _____ foods that his father used to make.

3. Mr. Ruiz decides to _____ a piñata to look like a donkey.

4. He adds long paper _____ to hang from the feet of the donkey.

5. Mr. Ruiz fills the piñata with a _____ of toys and treats.

EXTEND YOUR VOCABULARY

Dictionary Skills Words in a dictionary appear in alphabetical order.

▶ **Write each set of words in alphabetical order.**

6. | traditional | streamers | overlap |

a. _____

b. _____

c. _____

7. | fiesta | fringe | features |

a. _____

b. _____

c. _____

Focus Skill

Sequence

Writers can tell how to make or do something. They write the **steps** in the **sequence**, or order, in which they happen.

▷ **Use information from the article to complete the chart.**
Write the order of the steps to tell how to make a piñata.

Step 1 First, make the piñata frame.

Step 2 _____

Step 3 _____

Step 4 _____

Step 5 _____

▷ **Use the article and your chart to write the answers.**

1. What happens before the piñata is filled with treats?

_____

2. In which step do you need to use cardboard?

_____

Your Turn to Write

▷ **Think about something that you like to make. Use the chart below to show the sequence of the steps you take to make it.**

I like to make _____.

| Step 1 | _____ |

↓

| Step 2 | _____ |

↓

| Step 3 | _____ |

↓

| Step 4 | _____ |

↓

| Step 5 | _____ |

▷ **On a separate sheet of paper, write a paragraph that tells how to make something. Use the information from your chart to write the paragraph.**

Why Otters Live in Water

A Cherokee Folktale

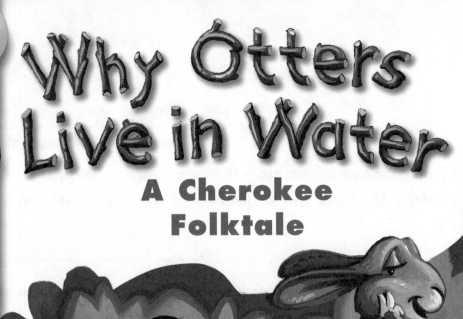

? What Do You Already Know?

Long ago, people told folktales to try to explain things that happened in nature. Think about a folktale you have read or heard. What did it try to explain?

VOCABULARY

council (KOWN suhl)
A group that makes decisions

celebration
(sel uh BRAY shuhn)
A special event or day

★ Get Ready to Read

When you make a **prediction**, you **guess** what will happen next. Story details often give clues about what may happen next. When you read the story, look for details that help you predict what will happen to Otter.

Many, many moons ago, Otter was an animal that would not go near the water. She was too proud of her silky, smooth fur to get it wet. Rabbit knew this about Otter. Rabbit also loved to play tricks. He made up his mind that one day he would teach Otter that she shouldn't be so proud of her coat.

One year, the great **council** of animals met. They decided they should honor the animal with the most beautiful fur. They would have a grand **celebration** with singing and dancing.

⭐ **Tip**

As you read, think about what you know about the characters. Make a prediction about what they will do **next**.

The great council sat around a fire and talked about the animals that had the best fur.

"What about Coyote?" asked Bear.

"The Fire Beings burned the tip of his tail," said Squirrel. "My fur is better than his!"

"What about Otter?" asked Frog while rolling her big eyes at Squirrel. "Otter's fur is really soft. It is glossy, too! You can't argue with that."

All the animals agreed. Otter had the most beautiful fur. The great council decided to honor Otter with a special celebration.

The council sent Rabbit to tell Otter about their choice. Rabbit was to bring Otter to the celebration. Since Rabbit ran so fast, he was often the **messenger** for the council. But Rabbit always liked to have some fun along the way.

⭐ **Tip**

Check your prediction. If your prediction was not correct, reread the **first part** of the story. If it was correct, make another prediction for the end of the story.

VOCABULARY

jealous (JEL uhs)
Wanting what someone else has

scheme (SKEEM)
A plan

overjoyed
(oh vuhr JOYD)
Very happy

exhausted
(eg ZAWS tud)
Very tired

As Rabbit ran past the forest, he thought of Otter's beautiful fur. He became very **jealous**. "I must think of a trick to get Otter's fur coat," Rabbit thought. Soon he had a **scheme**.

When Rabbit arrived at Otter's house, he put on a big smile and told Otter the news. Otter was **overjoyed**.

Immediately Rabbit and Otter started back. Rabbit took a much longer path on the return trip. He led Otter over the hills before going past the mountains and Rabbit's camp.

The sun began to set. Otter was tired. She sat down by a river. "I am too **exhausted** to go any farther. I think we should stop for the night."

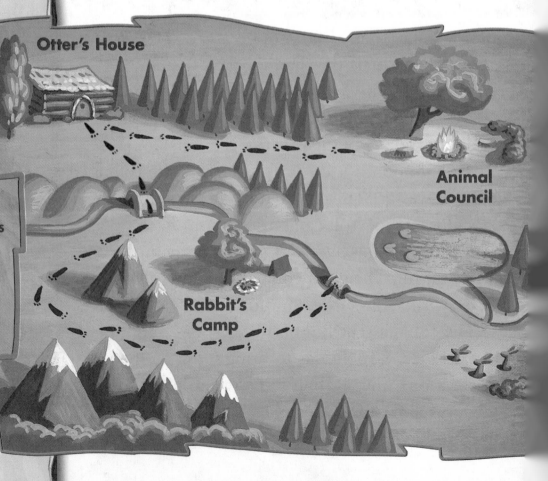

MAP KEY

🏔 Mountains
〰 River
•🔸• Path
🏕 Forest
⛰ Hills

Rabbit looked very serious. "We can stop. But this is a place where fire rain falls from the sky. I do not want your beautiful fur to be burned. Maybe you should take your fur off."

"But I will get cold!" cried Otter.

"Then I will build a campfire," said Rabbit.

Otter took off her fur coat and hung it on a tree branch. She decided she would slip into the water if the fire rain began to fall. Then she lay down next to the river and went to sleep.

A few minutes later, Rabbit tossed hot coals from the fire into the air. He began to shout, "Fire rain! Run for your life!"

Otter awoke and quickly dove into the water. She swam to the middle of the river. Rabbit grabbed Otter's beautiful fur coat and quickly scampered away with it.

Otter saw Rabbit take her coat. She knew she had been tricked. However, Otter found out that she enjoyed swimming in the water. She liked it so much that she stayed! That is why all otters live in water today. After awhile, Otter got her fur coat back. But that is another story!

scampered
(SKAM puhrd) Ran quickly

Comprehension Check

Answer the questions below in complete sentences.

1. Why was Rabbit often the messenger for the great council?

   _____

   _____

2. Why did Rabbit take Otter back a longer way?

   _____

   _____

3. Why did Otter take off her fur coat?

   _____

   _____

4. What did Rabbit do after Otter fell asleep?

   _____

   _____

5. Why do you think Rabbit was jealous of Otter's fur?

   _____

   _____

6. What might Otter have done to get her fur coat back?

   _____

   _____

▶ **Read the paragraph. Fill in the circle next to the word that completes each sentence.**

The animal _____ sat around a fire. They
      1
were planning a _____ that would last for three
      2
days. Rabbit was sent to invite all the animals. Bear watched
as Rabbit ran away to share the news. Bear wanted to be a
_____ , too. He was _____ that
      3   4
Rabbit had long legs. He wanted to run fast like Rabbit.

1. Ⓐ scheme
   Ⓑ couch
   Ⓒ council
   Ⓓ town

2. Ⓔ messenger
   Ⓕ camp
   Ⓖ house
   Ⓗ celebration

3. Ⓐ messenger
   Ⓑ singer
   Ⓒ swimmer
   Ⓓ dancer

4. Ⓔ surprised
   Ⓕ overjoyed
   Ⓖ jealous
   Ⓗ happy

EXTEND YOUR VOCABULARY

Synonyms Synonyms are words that have almost
the same meaning.

▶ **Circle the two words in each row that are synonyms.**

5.	scheme	map	plan	tribe
6.	happy	sad	overjoyed	silly
7.	hid	scampered	swam	ran
8.	lonely	exhausted	excited	tired

Make Predictions

Writers give clues in the story about what will happen next. These clues help readers make a **prediction**.

▶ **Use clues from the story to complete the chart.**

What I Predicted

Rabbit will try to get Otter's fur coat.

⬇

Clues That Helped Me Predict

1. Rabbit likes to play tricks.

2. _____

3. _____

⬇

What I Know Happened

_____

_____

▶ **Use the story and your chart to write the answers.**

1. Why do you think the author says that Rabbit likes to play tricks?

_____

_____

2. How did Rabbit get Otter to take off her fur coat?

_____

Your Turn to Write

▶ Choose an animal. Use the chart to plan a trick that Rabbit could play on your animal. The trick should explain why your animal looks or acts a certain way.

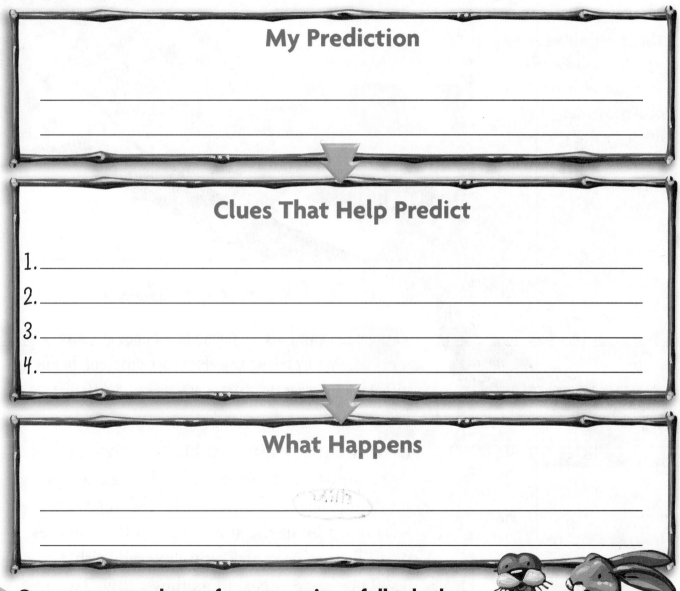

My Prediction

_____

_____

Clues That Help Predict

1. _____
2. _____
3. _____
4. _____

What Happens

_____

_____

▶ On a separate sheet of paper, write a folktale that tells why the animal you chose looks or acts the way it does. Use the information from your chart.

Weird and Wonderful Lizards!

Get Ready to Read

An article can **compare** by telling how things are alike. It can **contrast** by telling how things are different. In this article look for ways that lizards are alike and different.

There are many different kinds of lizards. But they are the same in some ways. All lizards are reptiles. Reptiles cannot keep themselves warm. Lizards often lie in the sun to warm their bodies. Also, all lizards have dry skin covered with **scales**. They **shed** this skin as they grow. Two weird and wonderful lizards are the frilled lizard and the veiled chameleon (kuh MEEL yuhn). Like all lizards, they both have scales and shed skin. They are also alike because they both live in trees.

veiled chameleon

★ **Tip**

Clue words such as same, alike, and both tell a reader that things are being compared.

VOCABULARY

predator
(PRED uh tuhr)
An animal that hunts other animals for food

camouflage
(CAM uh flazh)
Coloring or body parts that help an animal look like its surroundings

frilled lizard

Staying Alive

There are some big, hungry animals that like to eat lizards. A lizard is always watching for a **predator** that is looking for food. The frilled lizard and the veiled chameleon each have different body parts and different ways to keep themselves safe.

The frilled lizard gets its name from the flap of skin around its neck. The color of its skin looks like the tree trunks on which it lives. This special ability to blend in with the surroundings is called **camouflage**. Camouflage helps the frilled lizard hide from hungry predators.

If camouflage doesn't work, the frilled lizard has another way to protect itself. The frilled lizard opens its mouth very wide. Then the flap of skin opens like an umbrella around its head. This frilled flap makes the lizard look bigger than it really is.

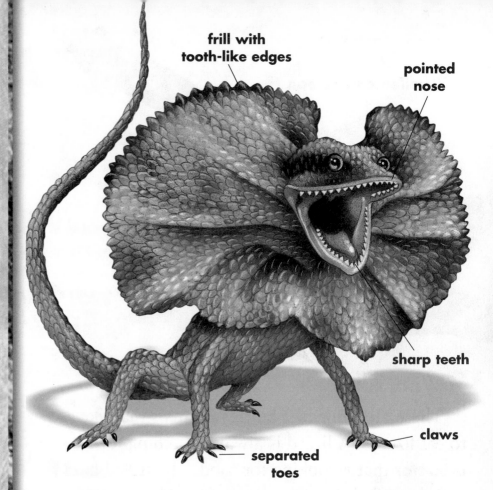

frill with
tooth-like edges

pointed
nose

sharp teeth

claws

separated
toes

**The bright, opened frill helps
the frilled lizard scare away danger.**

⭐ **Tip**

Clue words such as
different, unlike, but,
and however tell that
things are being
contrasted.

VOCABULARY

sway (SWAY) To move
back and forth

crest (KREST) Part of
an animal's body that
rises above its head

If the predator still does not go away, the
frilled lizard will stand on its two back legs and
sway from side to side. It beats its long tail on
the ground and jumps toward the predator. When
all else fails, the frilled lizard turns and runs away
on its back legs!

Unlike the frilled lizard, the veiled chameleon
moves very slowly. It does not have any body
parts that can scare away a predator. The veiled
chameleon does use camouflage to stay safe but
in a different way from the frilled lizard. Its body
is green with yellow, orange, and blue stripes.
It also has a crest on its head. When the veiled
chameleon sits in a tree, its body will shake like
a leaf blowing in the wind. It can hide from a
predator by blending in with the other leaves.

eyes that move in different directions

The veiled chameleon can change its color.

crest

long claws

long, curling tail

On the Hunt

The frilled lizard and the veiled chameleon both eat insects. But they have different ways to hunt for food. The frilled lizard is a fast runner. It sees a tasty treat and runs to catch it with its mouth. However, the veiled chameleon sits very still and watches. It is too slow to run. The chameleon's eyes can move in two different directions. One eye will look for its prey, while the other eye looks for danger.

When the veiled chameleon sees an insect, it slowly moves toward it. Its long toes help it grasp tree branches. It also has a long tail. When it walks or hunts for food, the veiled chameleon uses its tail to hold onto the tree branch. When the veiled chameleon is near its prey, its sticky tongue darts out to catch the insect!

There are many other weird and wonderful lizards. Each lizard has its own amazing ways to stay safe and hunt for food.

VOCABULARY

prey (PRAY) An animal that is hunted by another animal for food

grasp (GRASP) To take hold of

Comprehension Check

Fill in the circle next to the best answer.

1. Why do lizards lie in the sun?

   Ⓐ They have scales.
   Ⓑ They need a way to warm their bodies.
   Ⓒ The sun makes them shed their skin.
   Ⓓ They are reptiles.

2. What does the veiled chameleon do to keep safe?

   Ⓔ It runs away on its back legs.
   Ⓕ It opens its mouth very wide.
   Ⓖ It hides by looking like a leaf.
   Ⓗ It looks bigger than it really is.

3. The author wrote this article mainly to —

   Ⓐ entertain readers with a funny story about lizards
   Ⓑ ask readers to buy pet lizards
   Ⓒ tell about how chameleons change colors
   Ⓓ tell readers about two kinds of lizards

4. What would be another good title for this article?

   Ⓔ The Veiled Chameleon
   Ⓕ Two Amazing Lizards
   Ⓖ The Life of the Frilled Lizard
   Ⓗ All About Reptiles

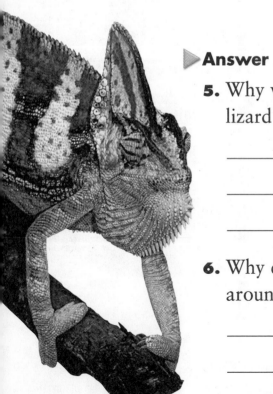

Answer the questions below in complete sentences.

5. Why would the open flap of skin on the frilled lizard scare away a predator?

   _____

   _____

   _____

6. Why do you think the veiled chameleon wraps its tail around a tree branch when it hunts for food?

   _____

   _____

   _____

Vocabulary Builder

▶ **Write the words from the box to complete the story.**

camouflage	crest	grasp	predator	prey	sway

A veiled chameleon was warming itself in the sun. Suddenly, it spotted a scary _____ looking for food. The
1
lizard did not want to be the bird's _____. The
2
chameleon slowly wrapped its tail around a tree branch. Then it used its long claws to _____ the branch. The
3
chameleon began to _____ slowly. With its
4
bright colors and the _____ on its head, the
5
chameleon looked just like a leaf. The chameleon had used _____ to save its life.
6

EXTEND YOUR VOCABULARY

Words That Have Two Meanings
Some words can have more than one meaning.

▶ **Read each word and its meanings. Write the letter of the meaning for each underlined word.**

scales a. Thin, flat plates that cover the body of some animals. **b.** Tools used to find out how much things weigh.

shed c. To lose or fall off naturally. **d.** A small building that is used to store things.

7. We looked for a hammer inside the tool <u>shed</u>. _____

8. The farmer used <u>scales</u> to weigh the fruit. _____

9. The young lizard was about to <u>shed</u> its skin. _____

10. The garden snake had smooth, dry <u>scales</u>. _____

Focus Skill

Compare and Contrast

Writers **compare** to show how two or more things are alike. They **contrast** to show how the things are different.

▶ **Use the article to fill in the diagram. Under each lizard's name, write details that tell about that lizard. Under "Both," write details that tell about both lizards.**

FRILLED LIZARD	BOTH	VEILED CHAMELEON
fast runner	scales	moves slowly

▶ **Use the article and your diagram to write the answers.**

1. Write two details that tell how the lizards are alike.

_____

_____

2. Write two details that tell how the lizards are different.

_____

_____

40 Comparing and Contrasting

Your Turn to Write

▷ **Choose either the frilled lizard or the veiled chameleon. Then choose another animal that you know about. Use the diagram below to compare and contrast the two.**

BOTH

▷ **On a separate sheet of paper, write a paragraph that compares and contrasts the lizard to the other animal. Use the information from your diagram.**

SNOWBALL
Is Missing!

? What Do You Already Know?

Have you ever lost something that belonged to you? What did you do to find it?

VOCABULARY

frisky (FRIS kee) Playful and full of energy

⭐ Get Ready to Read

Authors do not always tell readers everything. You can figure something out and **draw conclusions** by using story clues and by using what you already know. As you read, look for clues that could help find the missing cat.

Alex ran in the front door. Her best friend Sara followed behind. Sara was staying over for the weekend. "Mom, we're home!" Alex called.

"I'm in the kitchen making dinner," Mrs. Akido answered. "Are you girls hungry?"

The girls walked into the kitchen. Alex saw her cat's collar by the door. "Snowball lost her collar again. Do you know where she is, Mom?" asked Alex.

"I haven't seen Snowball lately," said Mrs. Akido. "I had to lock her out of my art studio earlier because she was too **frisky**. She kept jumping up on the table."

Alex and Sara searched for Snowball. They walked around the house shaking a box of Kitty Vittles and calling her name. There was no sign of Snowball.

The girls walked inside the art studio. "Oh no!" they groaned. Ink was splattered on the desk and there were paw prints everywhere.

"Look at the prints," said Sara. "They stop at the open window."

The girls ran outside. They looked everywhere. They shook the cat food box. They called Snowball's name. There was still no sign of her.

As the day grew late, Alex went to get a photo of Snowball. She scanned it on the computer and made "Missing" posters.

Alex and Sara hung the posters all over the neighborhood. But, soon it was dark and they had to return home. Alex felt **hopeless**.

"Now we have to start thinking like real **detectives**," Sara said. "Let's start by listing what we know about this case."

Alex made a list of clues in a notebook. "It's not much," she said with a sigh. "We'll start searching again tomorrow morning."

★ **Tip**

If you saw footprints that stopped at an open window, what conclusion **might** you draw?

Clues
1. Snowball's collar in the kitchen
2. Open window
3. Inky paw prints

VOCABULARY

hopeless (HOHP liss) Feeling like the worst will happen

detectives (dee TEK tivz) People who find information and solve crimes

★ **Tip**

When you read a story, stop to think about different conclusions that **make sense**.

VOCABULARY

lead (LEED) Helpful information; a clue

harmless (HARM liss) Not able to cause damage

Clues

1. Snowball's collar in the kitchen
2. Open window
3. Inky paw prints
4. Cat noises on Cottage Street
5. Garbage can tipped over
6. Tuna fish cans
7. Paw prints by the garbage can

The next morning, the girls woke to the sound of the phone ringing. Alex and Sara got dressed and ran downstairs.

"We may have a clue, girls," Dad said. "Mrs. Green on Cottage Street just called. Last night she heard cat noises. This morning she found her garbage can knocked over."

"Our first **lead**," Alex exclaimed. "Let's check it out!"

Alex and Sara went over to the scene. They looked at the garbage. Sara noticed that there were tuna cans and paw prints.

"Snowball must have been here," Sara said. She added more clues to their list. Then the girls looked closely at the prints. The prints looked like little hands.

"I don't think these are cat prints, but I'm not sure what they belong to," said Sara. "Yuck, do you smell something bad?"

"I know what the prints belong to," Alex whispered. "They belong to a skunk and it's right there."

"Be very quiet," said Sara backing slowly away. "They're **harmless** as long you don't scare them."

As soon as the animal walked away, the girls ran. They were **fearful** of getting sprayed. When they were home, the girls sat down on the front steps. The search was not **successful**, so they crossed off some clues.

"Any luck, girls?" Alex's dad asked. They shook their heads and told Mr. Akido what happened.

"That's strange," he said. "Skunks are **nocturnal**. They only come out at night."

Suddenly there was a flash of black and white in the bush. "Look," said Sara. "That skunk followed us. Get in the house!"

But Alex shook the box of Kitty Vittles. Sara watched in horror as the smelly animal came at them. But it wasn't a skunk after all.

"It's Snowball!" Sara cried. "Alex, how did you know?"

"First she got covered in ink and went out the window. Next she wandered off to Cottage Street," Alex explained. "Snowball was hungry, so she got into the tuna cans. The reason Snowball smells so bad is because a skunk sprayed her."

"Good work. But let's give Snowball a bath," laughed Sara. "Or you'll have to change her name to Stinkball!"

Clues

1. Snowball's collar in the kitchen
2. Open window
3. Inky paw prints
4. Cat noises on Cottage Street
5. ~~Garbage can tipped over~~
6. ~~Tuna fish cans~~
7. ~~Paw prints by the garbage can~~

VOCABULARY

fearful (FIHR fuhl) Afraid

successful (suk SES fuhl) Doing well

nocturnal (nok TUR nuhl) Active at night

✔ Comprehension Check

▶ **Answer the questions below in complete sentences.**

1. Why do you think the cat was named Snowball?

_____

_____

2. What problem did Alex and Sara have in the story?

_____

_____

3. Why did the girls think Snowball jumped out the window?

_____

_____

4. Where did the girls search after Mrs. Green called?

_____

_____

5. Why did Sara think Snowball was a skunk when she first saw her?

_____

_____

6. How do you think Alex and Sara felt after finding Snowball?

_____

_____

Vocabulary Builder

▶ **Fill in the circle next to the correct answer.**

1. In this story, <u>frisky</u> means—

  Ⓐ missing
  Ⓑ playful
  Ⓒ sad
  Ⓓ lost

2. In this story, <u>detectives</u> means—

  Ⓔ people who cook food
  Ⓕ people who write books
  Ⓖ people who paint
  Ⓗ people who find information

3. In this story, <u>nocturnal</u> means—

  Ⓐ something that eats garbage
  Ⓑ something that is active at night
  Ⓒ something that smells really bad
  Ⓓ something that is missing

4. In this story, <u>lead</u> means—

  Ⓔ metal
  Ⓕ follow
  Ⓖ clue
  Ⓗ show

EXTEND YOUR VOCABULARY

Suffixes A suffix is a word part that is added to the end of a word. A suffix changes the meaning of a word.

less = without	ful = full of

▶ **Circle the suffix in each word. Write the meaning of each word on the line.**

5. fearful   _____

6. harmless   _____

7. hopeless   _____

8. successful   _____

Draw Conclusions

Readers **draw conclusions** by thinking about clues or facts in a story and by using what they already know.

▶ **Fill in the chart. Write the clues that helped you draw conclusions.**

Clues from Reading

Snowball lost her collar.

_____

_____

_____

_____

What I Already Knew

A cat without a collar

might be lost.

_____

_____

_____

My Conclusion

_____

_____

▶ **Use the story and your chart to write the answers.**

1. Why didn't Sara recognize Snowball at first?

_____

2. How did Alex explain what happened to Snowball?

_____

_____

Your Turn to Write

▷ Think about something you have that is important to you.
Suppose it is missing. What could have happened to it?
What clues might help you find it?

Clues

_____

_____

_____

_____

_____

_____

What I Already Know

_____

_____

_____

_____

_____

_____

My Conclusion

_____

_____

_____

_____

_____

▷ On a separate sheet of paper, write a mystery story about
something that is missing. Use the information from your chart.

▶ **Read the story. Then answer the questions.**

Don't Look Down!

Nathan's hands shook as he strapped on the helmet. Then he slipped his arms and legs into the harness. He belted it tightly. Next the scout leader hooked a rope to the harness. The harness and rope would keep Nathan safe as he crossed the bridge.

Nathan looked at the bridge. It was a log laid across a river. Nathan really didn't like heights, but he was determined to make it. The log moved from side to side. Walking across the log bridge would be a big challenge.

Nathan grabbed the rope railing with one hand and stepped on the log. He tried not to look down. Nathan slid one foot, and then the other along the log. The bridge was very narrow. He slowly began to cross the river. He felt the wind blowing and the rush of the water below. Nathan thought he might have to turn back.

"You can do it!" Nathan's friends cheered. Then Nathan felt as if he might make it. When he was almost to the other side, Nathan took a deep breath. He had just a few steps left. Suddenly, he jumped off the log and yelled, "I did it!" Now that he had done it once, Nathan felt like he could walk across a million log bridges!

Fill in the circle next to the best answer.

1. What problem did Nathan face?

   (A) Belting on a harness
   (B) Building a bridge
   (C) Swimming across a river
   (D) Walking on a log bridge

2. What happened right after Nathan grabbed the rope railing?

   (E) He took a deep breath.
   (F) He strapped on the helmet.
   (G) He stepped on the log.
   (H) He jumped off the log.

3. Nathan's friends began to cheer—

   (A) after he put on his helmet
   (B) before he stepped on the log
   (C) as he crossed the river
   (D) after he crossed the river

4. Another good title for this story is—

   (E) Nathan's Big Challenge
   (F) How To Make a Log Bridge
   (G) All About Log Bridges
   (H) A Bridge in the Woods

Answer the questions in complete sentences.

5. Why was it a challenge for Nathan to cross the bridge?

   _____

   _____

6. How did Nathan change during the story?

   _____

   _____

   _____

Read the article. Then answer the questions.

The Eastern Bluebird

The eastern bluebird is known as a songbird. It is one of the most colorful birds. The male bluebird has dark blue on his head, back, wings, and tail. His throat and chest are a dull red color. The male's stomach is white. On the other hand, the female bluebird is mostly light gray. There may be some blue on her wings and tail, but it can be seen only when she is flying. The female's throat and chest are a mix of red and brown. The female bluebirds are not as colorful as males because they need to blend in with the nest when they sit on eggs.

Female eastern bluebirds lay four to six blue eggs. It takes about two weeks for the eggs to hatch. A male bluebird often brings food to a female that is sitting on eggs.

Bluebirds live in open fields where there are many kinds of grasses and bushes. The different plants provide a bigger variety of insects. It is easy for bluebirds to find insects where short plants grow. Bluebirds sit on a perch and dive to the ground when they see prey.

Fill in the circle next to the best answer.

1. How is a male bluebird different from a female bluebird?

   ○ The female has a dull red chest.
   ○ The female is all blue.
   ○ The male is more colorful.
   ○ The male has blue spots.

2. Why do female bluebirds "need to blend in"?

   ○ bright colors scare baby birds
   ○ so that they can hide from animals
   ○ so they can hide from insects
   ○ so they can find more insects

3. If a bluebird dives to the ground, what will probably happen next?

   ○ It will catch an insect.
   ○ It will lay eggs.
   ○ It will make a nest.
   ○ It will sing a song.

4. Why do you think it is easy for bluebirds to find insects where short plants grow?

   ○ Insects can't hide as easily.
   ○ Insects can't get caught in the plants.
   ○ Bluebirds can't see well.
   ○ Bluebirds can't fly.

Answer the questions in complete sentences.

5. How are the male bluebird and female bluebird different?

   _____

   _____

   _____

6. Suppose that a female bluebird leaves the nest after 13 days. What might have happened?

   _____

   _____

   _____

Save the Rain Forests!

Get Ready to Read

Nonfiction articles give **facts**. Facts are statements that can be proven to be true. Articles can also give **opinions**. Opinions are a person's feelings or beliefs. In this article look for facts and opinions about rain forests.

What is that strange sound? It's a howler monkey calling out a warning. See that furry animal moving in slow motion? That's a three-toed sloth. Welcome to the rain forest. You won't find a more interesting place anywhere else on Earth!

Most rain forests are found near the center of Earth, or the **equator**. This area is called the **tropics**. The weather stays hot all year round. Tropical rain forests usually get between 160 and 400 inches (400–1000 centimeters) of rain each year. The rain forests may be wet, but they're also bursting with life.

VOCABULARY

equator
(ee KWAY tuhr) The imaginary line around the center of Earth

tropics (TROP iks)
The very hot area near the equator, or center of Earth

Treetop Treasures

The top layer of trees in a rain forest is called the **canopy**. The canopy leaves are very **dense**. Almost no light reaches down to the floor of the rain forest because of this thick layer.

A rain forest canopy is one of the richest places on Earth. Almost half of the world's plant and animal **species** live in a jungle canopy.

How do scientists learn about rain forests? One way is by living in canopy rafts. Canopy rafts look like huge spider webs. Sometimes hot air balloons drop the rafts in place. Scientists must climb almost 100 feet (30 meters) up to get to the canopy rafts. They work and sleep in the rafts. From the rafts, scientists can get a good look at the canopy's plants and animals. They study how each one lives and grows.

★ Tip

When you read a statement, ask yourself, "Can this statement be proven?" If the answer is **yes**, it is a **fact**. If the answer is **no**, it is an **opinion**.

VOCABULARY

canopy (KAN uh pee)
A covering or top layer

dense (DENS)
Very thick

species (SPEE sheez)
Groups of living things that have some of the same features

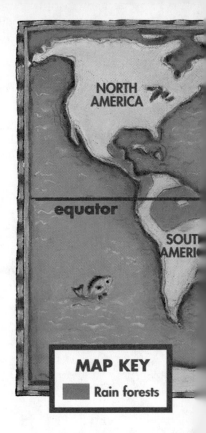

VOCABULARY

extinct (ex TINKT)
No longer living

destruction
(di STRUK shuhn)
The act of ruining
something

jaguar

Destroying Rain Forests

Rain forests are in trouble. Each day more and more of the rain forests are cut down or burned. You probably live far from a rain forest, so why should you care about them?

Rain forests are important to everyone on the planet. The plants in the rain forests make a gas in the air that we need to breathe. Rain forests also help control Earth's weather. When the trees are cut down, Earth gets hotter.

Trees are not the only things that are lost when rain forests are cut down. Many kinds of animals become **extinct**. Over 20,000 different kinds of plants and animals are destroyed each year.

We must end this **destruction**. We must share Earth with all plants and animals. I think it would be a sad world without the slow-moving sloth or the powerful jaguar.

NORTH AMERICA

equator

SOUTH AMERICA

MAP KEY

Rain forests

sloth

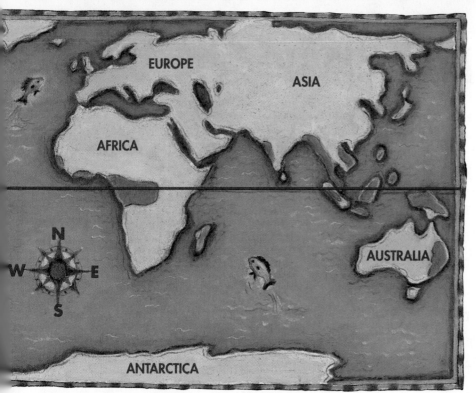

Tropical rain forests are found near the center of Earth.

periwinkle

The Outdoor Drugstore

For thousands of years, people have lived in the rain forests. These **native** people know how to use rain forest plants to keep healthy. They have learned how to use every part of the forest without destroying it. Many scientists now study with the native people of the rain forests to learn about the medicines that are found there.

It is a fact that over one fourth of our medicines come from plants. Many of these plants can be found only in rain forests. One important drug comes from a plant called periwinkle. This drug can help people who have leukemia (loo KEE mee ah) or Hodgkin's Disease.

Some people believe that the cures for many diseases may be found in rain forests. If we destroy them, we may never know. It is for this reason, and many more, that we must save the rain forests. In my view, our future depends on it.

Comprehension Check

Fill in the circle next to the best answer.

1. What is the main reason the author wrote this article?

   ○ to tell a funny story about rain forests

   ○ to ask readers to protect rain forests

   ○ to tell readers about the lives of rain forest animals

   ○ to ask readers to visit rain forests

2. How do scientists learn about rain forest medicines?

   ○ by studying with people who live in the rain forests

   ○ by collecting the rain that falls in the rain forests

   ○ by eating the plants

   ○ by watching the animals

3. Why do scientists live on canopy rafts?

   ○ The canopy rafts help them float in the water.

   ○ The canopy rafts help them study plants and animals.

   ○ The canopy rafts help them stay warm in the sunlight.

   ○ The canopy rafts help them swim.

4. What does not happen when rain forests are destroyed?

   ○ Trees are lost.

   ○ Animals become extinct.

   ○ We lose many medicines that could help cure diseases.

   ○ Scientists learn more about rain forest plants.

Answer the questions below in complete sentences.

5. Why are rain forests important to everyone on Earth?

   _____

   _____

6. What do you think will happen if rain forests continue to be cut down?

   _____

   _____

Vocabulary Builder

Write a word from the box for each clue. The boxed letters will spell the name of a rain forest bird.

canopy	destruction	equator	extinct	native

1. The imaginary line around the center of Earth
___ ___ ___ ___ [1] [2] ___

2. The act of ruining something
___ ___ ___ ___ ___ [3] ___ ___ ___ ___ ___

3. No longer living
___ ___ ___ ___ [4] ___ ___

4. People born in a certain place
___ [5] ___ ___ ___ ___

5. A covering or top layer
___ ___ [6] ___ ___ ___

___ ___ ___ ___ ___ ___
1 2 3 4 5 6

EXTEND YOUR VOCABULARY

Context Clues Context clues are words or sentences that will help you figure out the meaning of an unknown word.

Look for clues to help you complete each sentence. Write a word from the box on each line.

dense	species	tropics

6. The _____ leaves blocked out the sun.

7. In the winter, I wish I was in the warm, sunny _____.

8. Animals that belong to one _____ are all in the same special group.

Fact and Opinion

Facts are statements that can be proven. **Opinions** are a person's beliefs or feelings. Opinions cannot be proven.

▶ **Use the article to fill in the chart. In the first column, write sentences from the article. Decide if each sentence is a fact or an opinion. Then write a sentence to tell how you know.**

Sentence	Fact or Opinion	How I Know
1. You won't find a more interesting place anywhere else on Earth!	opinion	It is a belief that cannot be proved.
2. Most rain forests are found near the equator.		
3.		
4.		

▶ **Write one opinion that the writer has. Then explain why you think this is an opinion.**

5. The writer believes that _____

_____.

6. I think it is an opinion because _____

_____.

Your Turn to Write

▶ Choose another issue that you have opinions about. It could be something that you feel strongly about. Use the chart below to list facts and your opinions about the issue.

Sentence	Fact or Opinion
1. _____ _____	_____
2. _____ _____	_____
3. _____ _____	_____
4. _____ _____	_____

▶ On a separate sheet of paper, write a letter to your principal, mayor, or town newspaper about your issue. Use the information from your chart.

William on the Prairie

★ Get Ready to Read

The **setting** tells **where** and **when** the events happen in a story. In this story look for details about the setting to help you picture where and when the events take place.

July 28, 1862

Dear Diary,

Ma and Pa gave me two presents for my birthday. They gave me this diary and a slingshot. Pa showed me how to use the slingshot. We tried hitting a tree with some rocks. Pa said it takes a lot of practice and that I should be careful never to use it around people. He also said you must be ready for anything out here on the prairie. We're new here in Kansas and the going has been rough so far.

I spent the rest of my birthday making traps. Coyotes have been tracking our cattle. I dug some deep pits and covered them with branches. I'd like to teach those big, wild dogs a lesson.

William

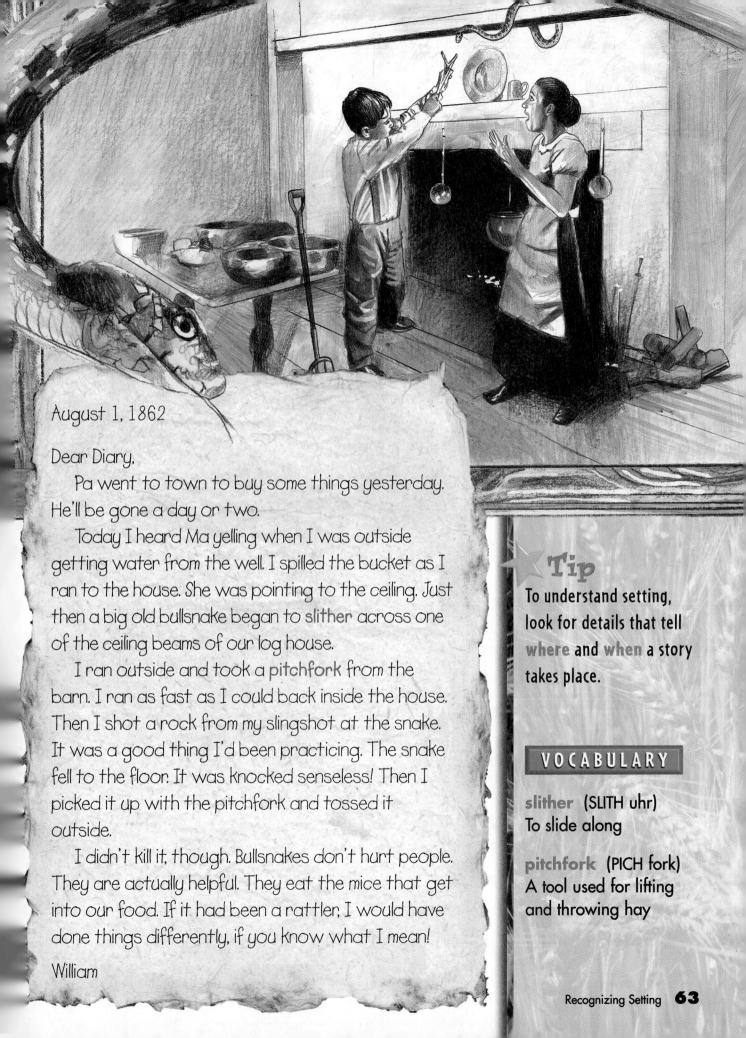

August 1, 1862

Dear Diary,

Pa went to town to buy some things yesterday. He'll be gone a day or two.

Today I heard Ma yelling when I was outside getting water from the well. I spilled the bucket as I ran to the house. She was pointing to the ceiling. Just then a big old bullsnake began to slither across one of the ceiling beams of our log house.

I ran outside and took a pitchfork from the barn. I ran as fast as I could back inside the house. Then I shot a rock from my slingshot at the snake. It was a good thing I'd been practicing. The snake fell to the floor. It was knocked senseless! Then I picked it up with the pitchfork and tossed it outside.

I didn't kill it, though. Bullsnakes don't hurt people. They are actually helpful. They eat the mice that get into our food. If it had been a rattler, I would have done things differently, if you know what I mean!

William

Tip
To understand setting, look for details that tell where and when a story takes place.

VOCABULARY

slither (SLITH uhr)
To slide along

pitchfork (PICH fork)
A tool used for lifting and throwing hay

Recognizing Setting **63**

Pay attention to the **words** that characters use for clues about the setting.

VOCABULARY

homestead
(HOME sted) A piece of land belonging to settlers

parched (PAR chd) Dry or thirsty

stampede
(stam PEED) People or animals making a sudden, wild rush in one direction

August 2, 1862

Dear Diary,

    A terrible fire came near our homestead the other day. We hadn't had any rain for weeks. All the prairie grass was bone dry. Instead of a sea of green grass, we had a sea of brown hay. The land was parched.

    My sister, Lillie, and I were out doing chores and watching the cattle. Suddenly, we saw licks of fire racing toward us. We had our herd dog lead the cattle past the farmhouse. The cattle made their way to safety in a great stampede. Then we had to save ourselves.

    I told Lillie to pull the branches away from one of the pits I had dug for the coyotes. Then we jumped inside. The fire burned right over the pit. I was sure glad that I hadn't caught a coyote in my trap!

    Luckily, the fire blew away from our farm without burning the house. Soon we were able to crawl out of the trap. We were hot and covered in soot from our hats to our boots. I reckon we were mighty lucky to be alive!

William

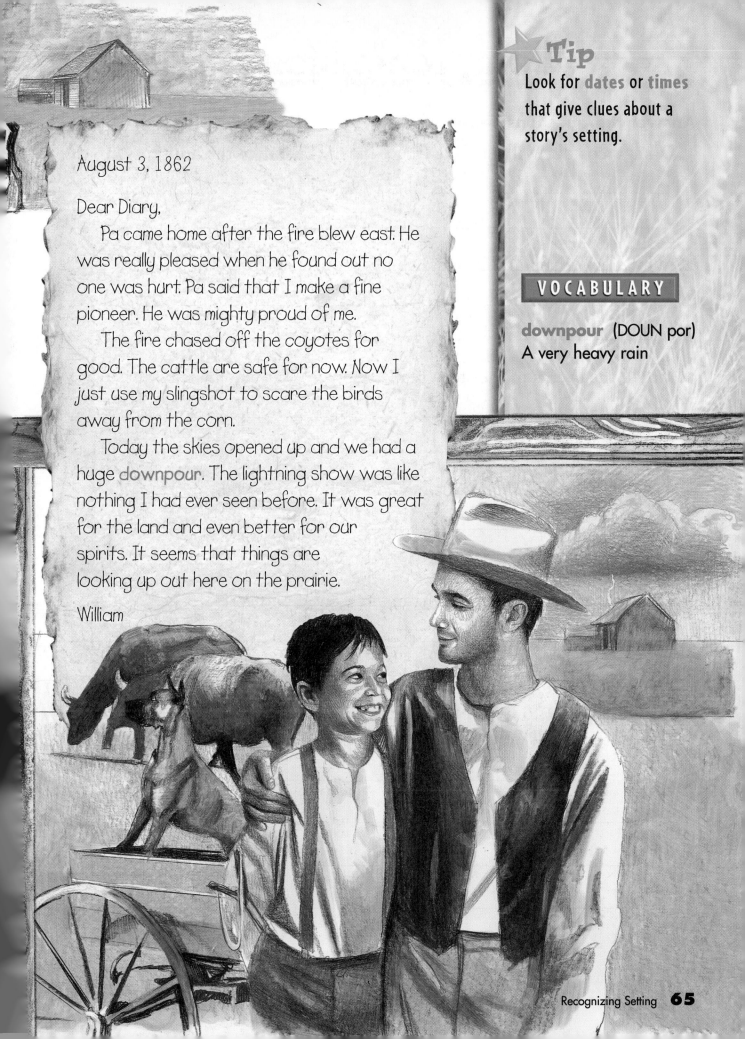

August 3, 1862

Dear Diary,

Pa came home after the fire blew east. He was really pleased when he found out no one was hurt. Pa said that I make a fine pioneer. He was mighty proud of me.

The fire chased off the coyotes for good. The cattle are safe for now. Now I just use my slingshot to scare the birds away from the corn.

Today the skies opened up and we had a huge downpour. The lightning show was like nothing I had ever seen before. It was great for the land and even better for our spirits. It seems that things are looking up out here on the prairie.

William

VOCABULARY

downpour (DOUN por)
A very heavy rain

Comprehension Check

▶Answer the questions below in complete sentences.

1. What steps did William take to get the snake out of the house?

_____

_____

2. Why did William and his sister jump into the coyote trap?

_____

_____

3. Could the events in the story really happen? Tell why or why not.

_____

_____

4. Why was William lucky that he didn't catch a coyote?

_____

_____

5. How did William show that he made a good pioneer?

_____

_____

6. Would you like to live in the time and place of the story? Tell why or why not.

_____

_____

_____

_____

Vocabulary Builder

Circle the letter next to the correct answer.

1. In this story, what does the word "tracking" mean?

   A. Running on a track
   B. Following an animal
   C. Reading a long book
   D. Writing in a diary

2. In this story, what does the word "stampede" mean?

   E. A postage stamp for a letter
   F. A dog that watches over cattle
   G. A sudden, wild rush of animals
   H. A home on the prairie

3. In this story, what does the word "parched" mean?

   A. Very dry
   B. Very wet
   C. Very tired
   D. Very green

4. In this story, what does the word "slither" mean?

   E. Bite and sting
   F. Scream and yell
   G. Fall down
   H. Slide along

EXTEND YOUR VOCABULARY

Compound Words A compound word is two words joined together to make a new word.

▶ **Put two words in the box together to fit each definition. Write the words on the lines.**

sling	fork	stead	pitch
down	shot	pour	home

5. A very heavy rain _____

6. A tool used for lifting hay _____

7. A large piece of land _____

8. A tool used for hitting targets _____

Setting

A story **setting** tells about **where** and **when** the story events take place.

▶ **Fill in the web to show the story's setting. Write details that tell where and when the story takes place.**

Setting

Detail

_____
_____
_____

Where
A pioneer farm
in Kansas

Detail

_____
_____
_____

Detail

_____
_____
_____

When

_____
_____

Detail

_____
_____
_____

▶ **Use the story and your web to write the answers.**

1. Describe where William lived.

_____
_____

2. How might William's diary be different if this story was set today?

_____
_____

Your Turn to Write

▶ **Think of a good setting for another story. Write details about the setting on the web below.**

Detail

_____

_____

_____

_____

Setting

Where

_____

_____

_____

_____

When

_____

_____

_____

Detail

_____

_____

_____

_____

Detail

_____

_____

_____

Detail

_____

_____

_____

▶ **On a separate sheet of paper, write a diary entry like one William wrote. Use details from your web to create the setting.**

Lighter Than Air

Get Ready to Read

When you **summarize**, you state the most important ideas from an article. Think about the most important ideas in each section as you read about skateboarding.

Have you ever wanted to fly? Well, just give Tony Hawk a skateboard and a ramp and he'll show you how.

Tony Hawk is one of the most famous skateboarders in the world. In his eighteen-year **career**, he has won more contests than anyone else has. Tony Hawk has invented over fifty tricks. His tricks include the *Switcheroo to Fakie* and the *360 Frontside Rock n' Roll*. Tony is also famous for skating a full loop. That means skating on a ramp that goes upside down!

It all began when Tony was nine years old. His brother gave him a skateboard. It was love at first skate.

Today, skateboarders all over the world try to **imitate** his smooth moves.

★ Tip

A summary should only include the most important ideas. What are the most important ideas in this section?

Practice Makes Perfect

Young Tony was so thin that regular knee pads didn't fit him. He had to wear elbow pads on his knees. That didn't stop him, though. Tony spent every minute at his local park in southern California. He learned from his brother and his friends. Soon, Tony was better than they were!

Tony **competed** in many contests. Sometimes Tony would be upset even if he won. "If I don't do my best, it kills me," he would say. Tony practiced more.

Tony's family **supported** his skateboarding. His dad helped start the National Skateboard Association. They set up more contests. They invited skaters from around the U.S. to compete. Skateboarding was finally getting noticed by people. Tony was also getting noticed. When he was twelve, a company started giving him free skateboards. After that, Tony's life began to change.

VOCABULARY

competed (kuhm PEET id) Took part in a contest

supported (suh PORT id) Helped and believed in someone

Skateboarding Pays Off

Soon skateboard companies started to offer Tony money to skate. Tony became a **professional** skateboarder when he was fourteen years old. By the time he was sixteen, Tony was the best skateboarder in the world.

Tony had earned so much money by the time he turned seventeen that he bought his own house. The first thing he did was to build some ramps in his yard.

As a professional, Tony Hawk competed in nearly every major contest. He won a record amount of awards. He placed in the top three in almost every contest he entered. Tony ruled the sport.

elbow pad

knee pad

helmet

★ **Tip**
A **summary** should be **short** and to the point.

VOCABULARY

professional
(proh FESH uh nuhl)
Making money for a job

TONY'S CAREER

AGE **9** TONY GETS HIS FIRST SKATEBOARD.

12 TONY GETS FREE SKATEBOARDS.

14 TONY TURNS PROFESSIONAL.

16 TONY IS THE BEST SKATEBOARDER IN THE WORLD.

17 TONY BUYS A HOUSE.

31 TONY COMPLETES A 900 AND RETIRES.

72 Summarizing

The **highlight** of his career was in 1999 at the ESPN X Games. It was there that he was the first, and still the only, person to complete a trick called the *900*. In this trick, Tony launches into the air, grabs his board, and spins around two and a half times while still in the air. At the X Games, Tony tried ten times to do the *900*. He finally made it on the eleventh try. No one else has been able to do it since!

For the Love of the Sport

Tony **retired** from professional skateboarding in 1999. He was thirty-one years old. Just because Tony's professional career is over, it doesn't mean his work is done. He continues to support the sport that helped him get where he is today. He hopes to bring the joy of skateboarding to more people each year.

He gives much of his time to building public parks for skateboarders. Tony believes that skateboarding helps build **confidence**. It upsets him that skateboarders are often yelled at and even punished for practicing what they love to do.

Tony also has a company called Birdhouse Projects. Birdhouse makes and sells skateboards, wheels, and clothes.

Tony hasn't hung up his skateboard, either. To help get people interested in the sport, Tony tours the world, skating in parks. He doesn't skateboard for money or prizes anymore. He does it for the love of the sport.

Tony Hawk doing one of his tricks

⭐ **Tip**

Look for the most important ideas from the **beginning, middle,** and **end** of an article.

VOCABULARY

highlight (HY lyt)
The best part of something

retired (ree TYRD)
Stopped working

confidence (KON fuh duhns)
A belief in yourself and your abilities

Comprehension Check

▶ **Fill in the circle next to the best answer.**

1. What made Tony Hawk start skateboarding?

   Ⓐ He wanted to start a skateboard company.
   Ⓑ He wanted to show off.
   Ⓒ He was given a skateboard as a gift.
   Ⓓ He took lessons from his brother.

2. How old was Tony when he became a professional?

   Ⓔ nine years old
   Ⓕ twelve years old
   Ⓖ fourteen years old
   Ⓗ sixteen years old

3. What is the main reason the author wrote this article?

   Ⓐ to ask readers to learn about skateboarding
   Ⓑ to tell readers about a famous person
   Ⓒ to entertain readers with a funny story
   Ⓓ to teach readers some tricks

4. What made Tony Hawk become so famous?

   Ⓔ He started skating when he was nine years old.
   Ⓕ He was the best skateboarder in the world.
   Ⓖ He started a company.
   Ⓗ He earned a lot of money.

▶ **Answer the questions below in complete sentences.**

5. What were the main reasons Tony Hawk was so successful?

   _____

   _____

   _____

6. Why do you think Tony Hawk retired when he was still young?

   _____

   _____

   _____

► **Write the word from the box that belongs with each group.**

| career | confidence | highlight | imitate | professional |

1. great moment, best day, _____

2. feeling good, pride, _____

3. jobs, work, _____

4. expert, getting paid, _____

5. copy, mimic, _____

EXTEND YOUR VOCABULARY

Words with Inflected Endings Many words end with *–ed.*
This ending can show that something happened in the past.

► **Write the word from the box that best completes each sentence.**

| compete | competed | retire | retired | support | supported |

6. Would you like to _____ in a contest?

Tony Hawk _____ when he was young.

7. I really _____ building new skate parks.

Tony's parents _____ his skateboarding career.

8. Tony _____ from skateboarding when he was young.

Most people _____ when they are much older.

Summarize

When you **summarize**, you tell the most important ideas from each part of an article or story.

▷ **Use the information from the article to fill in the chart. Write the most important ideas from each part of the article.**

 BEGINNING

Tony Hawk started skateboarding when he was young.

 MIDDLE

_____

_____

 END

_____

_____

▷ **Use the article and your chart to write a summary of the article.**

SUMMARY

_____

_____

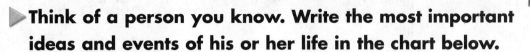

Your Turn to Write

▶ Think of a person you know. Write the most important ideas and events of his or her life in the chart below.

_____
_____
_____

_____
_____
_____

_____
_____
_____

▶ On a separate sheet of paper, write a summary of the person's life. Use the information from your chart.

_____
_____
_____

Let's Get Connected

What Do You Already Know?

How do you keep in touch with people who live far away? How would life be different if these things didn't exist?

Get Ready to Read

An **effect** is something that happens. A **cause** is the reason why it happens. In this article look for the effects that some things have had on our lives and what caused them to happen.

VOCABULARY

technology
(tek NOL uh jee)
The use of science to make life easier

inventions
(in VENT shuhnz)
Things created that did not exist before

Imagine what your life would be like if you never left your town. Then imagine that you talked only to people who lived within walking distance. If you lived two hundred years ago, that's probably what your life would have been like.

Many things have changed in the past two hundred years. New **technology** has brought people together. Two hundred years ago, it would have taken three weeks for a message to travel from San Francisco to New York. Today, you could deliver the same message in a matter of seconds! Our world seems much smaller today thanks to some important **inventions**.

Keep in Touch!

In 1860, the Pony Express was the fastest way to get a letter from coast to coast. Messengers riding horses would take about ten days to cross the country. As a result, **communication** between the east and west was better than it was before.

The Pony Express went out of business in a short time. This was partly because of the railroad. A train could carry letters just as quickly. It was also because of the telegraph. The telegraph used a code of dots and dashes. Operators tapped out the code. Then it traveled across wires **instantly**.

How Long a Letter Takes to Cross the U.S.

21 days
14 days
7 days

1860 Regular Mail | 1860 Pony Express | 2002 Regular Mail | 2002 Express Mail

Tip
Look for clue words and phrases such as because, so, and as a result. They signal causes and effects.

Morse Code for Telegraphs

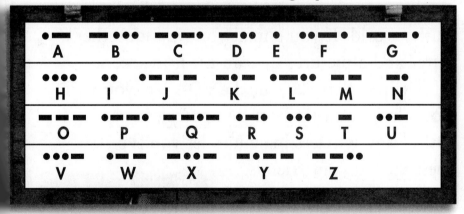

A B C D E F G
H I J K L M N
O P Q R S T U
V W X Y Z

All **rapid** communication was done by telegraph until 1876. Then Alexander Graham Bell invented the telephone. We can now chat with friends anywhere in the world because of his invention. The invention of the telephone also opened the door for walkie-talkies, radio, and even the Internet.

VOCABULARY

communication
(kuh MYOO ni kay shuhn)
Sharing information and ideas by talking or writing

instantly (IN stuhnt lee)
Happening right away

rapid (RAP id)
Very fast

1844
Morse sends first public telegraph message

1876
first telephone call

1973
Internet first links computer networks

It's a Small World

The telephone has come a long way since the days of Alexander Graham Bell. Today, wireless telephones have made it possible to talk to people just about anywhere. People can call each other from home, from a car, or from the middle of the desert. People can even use special telephones to call from airplanes thousands of feet above the ground.

The Internet is another amazing invention. The Internet allows millions of different computers to **network** and share information. Now you can send instant messages to people who live anywhere in the world. If you e-mail your grandmother a letter and a picture, she can get it in seconds.

A wireless **device** called a PDA lets you write notes by hand that your computer can read. Other tiny wireless machines let you type messages to your friends. The result is that people can communicate with others all of the time, from anywhere in the world!

You can write notes on a PDA.

★ Tip

Sometimes an effect has more than one cause. Sometimes a cause has more than one effect.

VOCABULARY

network (NET wurk)
To connect computers so they can work together

device (di VYSSE)
A machine that does a certain job

1830
first passenger
train in U.S.

1893
first
motorcar

1903
Wright Brothers take
first airplane flight

1969
first trip to
the moon

Moving Right Along!

Communication and transportation go hand in hand. Transportation inventions have also helped bring our world closer together. The best way to travel in the 1800s was by train. Railroads connected many parts of the United States. Then in the early 1900s, cars became a part of the American lifestyle. Suddenly, people could get places without walking, or horses, or days of travel.

In 1903, the Wright brothers flew the first modern airplane. Their plane stayed in the air only for a few seconds. Air travel has improved since their first flight.

Today, special airplanes can fly even at the speed of sound. This means we can travel from New York to Europe in just three hours! Air travel has become so advanced that space shuttles make trips to space stations and travel around Earth. Inventions in communication and transportation have brought our world closer together. Maybe someday, they will bring our whole universe together.

Tip

Sometimes writers don't include clue words. To find a cause, ask yourself, "Why did this happen?" To find an effect, ask yourself, "What happened?"

VOCABULARY

transportation
(TRANS pur TAY shuhn)
A way of moving from place to place

From New York City
3000 miles
(4828 kilometers)
to Paris

Answer the questions below in complete sentences.

1. What are some inventions that have changed communication?

_____

_____

2. How have wireless telephones changed our lives?

_____

_____

3. What do you use to communicate today that people two hundred years ago didn't have?

_____

_____

4. What is most likely the author's main purpose for writing this article?

_____

_____

5. What is an example of an opinion in this article?

_____

_____

6. Use the chart on page 79 to write your name in Morse code.

_____

_____

Vocabulary Builder

▶ **Fill in the circle next to the best answer.**

1. In this article, <u>device</u> means—

○ train
○ space
○ crime
○ machine

2. To <u>network</u> computers is to—

○ carry them
○ use them
○ type on them
○ connect them

3. <u>Inventions</u> means—

○ traveling from place to place
○ things created that did not exist before
○ things used to connect computers
○ planes that travel at the speed of sound

4. In this article, <u>rapid</u> means—

○ slow
○ quick
○ tired
○ pretty

5. In this article, <u>instantly</u> means—

○ right away
○ later on
○ inventing
○ inside

6. <u>Technology</u> means—

○ using special codes
○ using a telegraph
○ using science to make life easier
○ using horses to deliver letters

EXTEND YOUR VOCABULARY

Root Words If you know the meanings of root words, you can learn the meanings of other words.

▶ **Write the correct vocabulary word on each line.**

7. to move or carry + the act of = the act of moving or carrying

transport + ation = _____

8. to share ideas + the act of = the act of sharing ideas

communicate + tion = _____

Cause and Effect

A **cause** is why something happens. An **effect** is what happens.

▶ **Use the information from the article to fill in the chart. Write the inventions under "Cause." Write each effect under "Effect."**

Cause	Effect
The telegraph became widely used.	People could send coded messages instantly.
Wireless phones were invented.	
The Internet was invented.	
	People can travel to far away places in hours.

▶ **Use the article and your chart to write the answers.**

1. Why did the Pony Express go out of business?

_____

_____

2. What effect do the inventions in this article have in common?

_____

Your Turn to Write

▷ **Think about another invention that has caused changes in the way people live. Then write the effects of this invention.**

Cause	Effects
The _____ was invented.	_____ _____ _____ _____ _____ _____ _____ _____ _____ _____ _____

▷ **On a separate sheet of paper, write a paragraph about the invention. Use the information from your chart.**

Libby to the Rescue!

Get Ready to Read

A **character** is a person or animal in a story. Readers can learn about a character from clues in the story. Think about what Libby says and does in this story to find out what she is like.

Libby's mom and dad had just left for the night. They had jet-packed across the center of Pod Circle to watch the latest videos from Earth. As usual, Libby was left in charge of her younger brother and baby sister.

The space weather report had warned her of **meteor** showers. Libby's parents told her to call them if there were any problems.

Libby was helping Ben with his homework when the storm started. First it **pelted** the windows with meteor pieces. Then it hammered the roof. Suddenly, the lights went out!

★ **Tip**

Pay attention to what the main character **says**, **thinks**, and **does**.

VOCABULARY

gravity (GRAV uh tee) The force that pulls things down and keeps them from floating into space

oxygen (OK si juhn) A gas found in the air that people need to breathe

navigate (NAV uh gayt) To find a way to go

Libby was surprised. This was not supposed to happen! Why wasn't the backup power supply on? She picked up the skyphone to call her parents. The line was dead.

"What's going on, Libby?" Ben asked.

Libby was worried, but she stayed calm. "It's okay, Ben. It's just a meteor storm," she said. "Strap on your boots and get the baby. The pod is about to lose **gravity**."

Libby found a spare battery and tried to connect it to the space pod's power supply. No luck! Just then, the pod lost gravity. Things began to float around all over the pod. *This could get serious,* Libby thought. Without power, the **oxygen** pump will fail. The water machine will stop at the same time. Libby had to think quickly.

Luckily, Libby's parents had trusted her enough to give her the code to the spare jet packs. If she had to, Libby could help her brother and sister get into their packs. Then she could tie them to her own pack. Libby had learned how to **navigate** around Pod Circle on her own. They could jet to the sky patrol office for help.

While you are reading a story, **ask yourself**, "What will this character do next? Why do I think so?"

VOCABULARY

recharge (ree CHARJ)
To put power back in

disable (dis AY buhl)
To take away the ability to do something

Libby grabbed some ice cubes out of the freezer and placed them in the baby's bottle. When the ice melted, the baby would have something to drink. Libby was careful to strap down large objects so they wouldn't fly around the pod.

The family's Robopet would be fine, even without air or water. If his battery wore down, she could **recharge** him later.

That gave Libby an idea. Maybe she could use the robopet's battery to keep the family's pod running for a little while. She would have to distract him or he would think she wanted to play catch. Then he definitely wouldn't hold still.

"Ben," Libby told her brother, "I want you to rub Robo's belly. I need to sneak up behind him and **disable** his battery pack."

Libby's Pod

Water System

Libby's Room

Battery

Sky Phone

Kitchen

Ben listened carefully to his sister. Libby held her breath and tiptoed up behind Robo. In a flash, she grabbed the battery and plugged it into the pod's energy unit.

For a moment, Libby was **uncertain** about what was going to happen. She thought they might have to stick to her first plan. Then the lights came on. The fan started to move. Libby took a deep breath of the oxygen that flooded into the room.

Libby and Ben took off their gravity boots. Then they put the things that had floated away back in their places. She and Ben had just settled back into doing homework when their parents burst through the front door. They were still in their jet packs.

"Kids!" they called. "We had a scary power outage. Are you all okay?"

"We were just fine," said Libby with a smile. Libby and Ben slapped hands under the table. *Sometimes*, Libby thought, *there is just no need to worry your parents.*

Tip

Notice how the other **characters** act toward the **main character** and what they say about him or her.

VOCABULARY

uncertain (un SUR tun)
Not sure

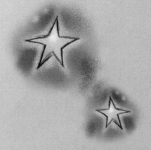

▶**Fill in the circle next to the best answer.**

1. What is the setting of this story?

   Ⓐ a home in space in the future
   Ⓑ a family home in the present
   Ⓒ a family home in the past
   Ⓓ a space station in the present

2. The author's purpose is most likely —

   Ⓔ to explain what to do when the power goes out
   Ⓕ to ask readers to live in space
   Ⓖ to entertain readers with a funny story
   Ⓗ to tell readers about life in a real space station

3. Libby had to act quickly because —

   Ⓐ she wasn't old enough to babysit
   Ⓑ she wasn't supposed to have the code to the jet packs
   Ⓒ the Robopet would cause trouble if she left him alone
   Ⓓ the pod would soon run out of air and water

4. What caused the power to go out?

   Ⓔ The batteries were old.
   Ⓕ A meteor shower hit the space pod.
   Ⓖ The power cord was unplugged.
   Ⓗ Libby forgot to recharge the batteries.

▶**Answer the questions below in complete sentences.**

5. What problems did Libby have that are like problems you might face?

   _____

   _____

6. How is the space pod different from your home today?

   _____

   _____

▶ **Write the words from the box to complete the story.**

gravity	meteor	navigate	oxygen	pelted

Terry was ready for his space walk. First he hooked up his hose that

gave him _____ to breathe. Then he strapped on his jet pack
           1

so he could _____ the way. As he floated out of the station,
           2

Terry did a flip. It was easy without _____. Suddenly, he
                                      3

saw a _____ shower in the distance. Some small rocks
       4

_____ Terry's spacesuit. He rushed back to
       5

the station. Terry would have to wait for another day.

EXTEND YOUR VOCABULARY

Prefixes **A prefix is a word part that is added to the beginning of a word. A prefix changes the meaning of the base word.**

re = to do again	un = not	dis = the opposite of

▶ **Add the correct prefix to each base word. Write the new word on the line to complete the sentence.**

able	certain	charge

6. Tim was _____ about what to do.

7. His dad told him to _____ the pod's battery.

8. They would _____ it and put it back in the pod.

Character

A **character** is a person or animal who is in a story. Readers can learn about a character from clues that tell what a character says or does.

▶ **Use the information from the story to fill in the chart.**

WHAT LIBBY IS LIKE	STORY CLUES
Libby thinks quickly.	She had the idea to use the battery from the Robopet.

▶ **Use the story and your chart to write the answers.**

1. How would you describe Libby?

_____

_____

2. Would you like to be friends with Libby? Tell why or why not.

_____

_____

Your Turn to Write

▶ **Think of a character such as a movie star or a sports star. Write what your character is like. Then write what your character says and does.**

WHAT _____ IS LIKE	CLUES

▶ **On a separate sheet of paper, write a story about your character. Use the information from your chart.**

Bringing Back the Bison

Get Ready to Read

Most authors write to **explain**, **entertain**, or **persuade** their readers. This is called the **author's purpose** for writing. Try to figure out the author's purpose as you read this article.

Have you ever seen a buffalo? American buffalo, or **bison**, are the largest land animals in North America. They have huge heads and horns. They have thick, dark fur on their backs. They also have long tails and short legs. An adult bison can weigh 2000 pounds (900 kilograms)!

Most people have never seen a bison up close. That's because real bison are not a common sight today. They were once an important part of our land, but they nearly died out. Today, people are working to help bison make a **comeback**. We can learn a lot from the story of these amazing animals.

There was once a large area in North America where bison lived.

A Great Beast at Risk

Long ago, many bison **roamed** the Great Plains. There were as many as 60 million bison in North America. Giant **herds** covered the plains and stopped trains in their tracks. However, by 1902 there were only 23 bison left in the entire United States.

What happened to them? As people began moving west, they settled on some of the land where the bison once lived. People also hunted the bison for meat and hides. Others hunted them for sport.

Organized groups of hunters often killed up to 250 bison a day. Train companies gave tourists the chance to shoot bison from their windows. There were even bison-killing contests. In one, a hunter set a record by killing 120 bison in just 40 minutes.

Tip

As you read, pay attention to the **headings** before each section. They can help you figure out the author's purpose.

VOCABULARY

roamed (ROHMED) Wandered

herds (HURDZ) Large groups of animals

Bison and the Native Americans

As the bison were being killed off, the Native Americans of the Great Plains were greatly affected. They depended on the bison. The bison were their most important **resource**. The Native Americans had great respect for the bison. Unlike the greedy hunters, Native Americans killed only as many animals as they needed. They used almost every part of the animal. Nothing was wasted.

Native Americans used bison meat for food. They made blankets, buckets, and snowshoes from bison hides. They used the skins to make clothing and **tepees**, or tents. They even made strings for their hunting bows from bison **sinews**.

Native American Uses for Bison

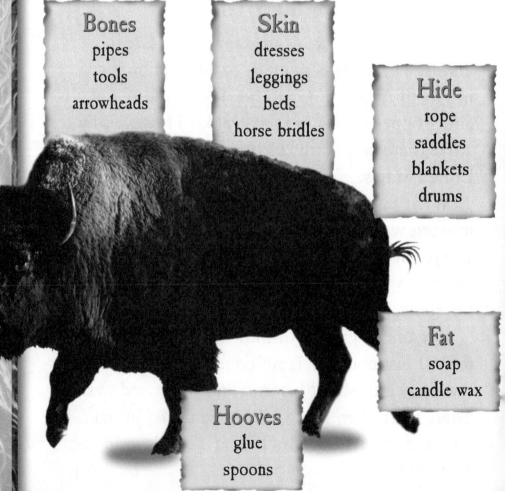

Bones
pipes
tools
arrowheads

Skin
dresses
leggings
beds
horse bridles

Hide
rope
saddles
blankets
drums

Horns
arrow tips
toys

Hair
pillows
rope
doll stuffing

Hooves
glue
spoons

Fat
soap
candle wax

YELLOWSTONE NATIONAL PARK

Almost Lost . . . and Found

When the bison were almost wiped out, some people began to try and save them. President Grant created Yellowstone National Park in 1872. He wanted to make a place where animals could be safe. Later, people created other **preserves** for animals like the bison. Laws were also passed to protect the bison from hunters. It became illegal for hunters to shoot bison for sport.

Their work has paid off. Now there are more than 10,000 bison in the United States. People are still working to keep the bison safe.

We can learn a lot from what happened to the bison. People almost caused these amazing animals to die out. But people also helped bring them back. Now we know there are many ways to protect other animals before they disappear.

Tip

The author sums up an **argument** in the last paragraph of the article. Read this paragraph again to make sure that you understand an argument.

VOCABULARY

preserves (pree ZERVZ) Places where plants and animals are protected

Comprehension Check

Answer the questions below in complete sentences.

1. What do bison look like?

_____

_____

2. Where in North America did the bison live?

_____

_____

3. Why did people kill the bison?

_____

_____

4. List four ways that Native Americans used the bison.

_____

_____

5. How did Native Americans show respect for the bison?

_____

_____

6. What would have happened if people did not try to protect the bison?

_____

_____

_____

_____

_____

Vocabulary Builder

▶ **Circle the letter next to the correct meaning for each underlined word.**

1. important <u>resource</u>

   A. something people throw away

   B. something people avoid

   C. something people use

   D. protected area

2. giant <u>herds</u>

   E. groups of animals

   F. noisy people

   G. bison

   H. groups of hunters

3. set up <u>tepees</u>

   A. tables

   B. tents

   C. fences

   D. beds

4. long <u>sinews</u>

   E. body parts

   F. national parks

   G. noses

   H. reports

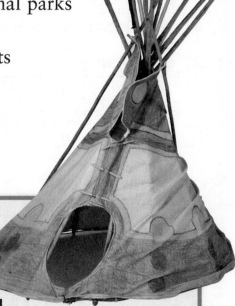

EXTEND YOUR VOCABULARY

Synonyms Synonyms are words that mean the same thing or nearly the same thing.

▶ **Read each sentence. Write a vocabulary word that is a synonym for each underlined word.**

bison	comeback	preserves	roamed

5. <u>Buffalo</u> live in many western states.   _____

6. Long ago, they <u>wandered</u> freely on the plains.   _____

7. Now they live mostly in wildlife <u>parks</u>.   _____

8. The bison have made a <u>return</u>.   _____

Author's Purpose

An **author's purpose** is the reason for writing. Some common purposes are to explain, to entertain, and to persuade.

▷ **Use the information from the article to fill in the chart. Write facts and examples from the article that helped you figure out the author's purpose.**

Author's Purpose

The author's purpose
is to explain what
happened to bison.

_____

_____

_____

_____

_____

Facts and Examples

_____

_____

_____

_____

_____

_____

_____

▷ **Answer the questions below in complete sentences.**

1. Tell why the author thinks it is important to save the bison.

_____

_____

2. Did the author persuade you? Tell why or why not.

_____

_____

Your Turn to Write

▷ **Think of something you want to persuade others to believe. Write the purpose and the reasons that will help persuade readers to agree with you.**

Author's Purpose

I want to persuade
readers to
_____
_____
_____
_____
_____
_____
_____
_____
_____
_____

Facts and Examples I Will Include

_____
_____
_____
_____
_____
_____
_____
_____
_____
_____
_____

▷ **On a separate sheet of paper, write a paragraph that is meant to persuade. Use the information from your chart to write your paragraph.**

▶ **Read the article. Then answer the questions.**

Land of the Dragons

Do you think dragons are just fire-breathing beasts from fairy tales? Actually, one kind of dragon is living today. You can find this real-life dragon on a small island called Komodo. The Komodo dragon doesn't breathe fire. It doesn't have wings. However, the Komodo dragon is still an amazing animal.

The Komodo dragon is the world's largest lizard. It can grow to be 10 feet (3 meters) long. It has rough, scaly skin. The dragon has a long neck and a tail that is longer than its body. Its feet have strong, sharp claws. The Komodo has large, sharp teeth that look like a saw.

The Komodo dragon is a fierce hunter. It hunts for prey such as deer, boars, and goats. The Komodo dragon has the strangest way of tracking down animals. When the dragon walks, it swings its head from side to side. The dragon uses its long, yellow tongue to taste the air. This helps it smell all around for food.

In spite of its size and power, the Komodo is now in danger of dying out. People have hunted the dragon for sport and destroyed some of the land where it lives. The Komodo is now protected by law. People must be careful to protect this huge reptile. We would not want dragons to only be in fairy tales.

▶ **Circle the letter next to the best answer.**

1. Which of the following statements is a fact?

  A. However, the Komodo dragon is still an amazing animal.

  B. People must be careful to protect this huge reptile.

  C. The dragon has a long neck and a tail longer than its body.

  D. The Komodo dragon has the strangest way of tracking down animals.

2. Which of the following statements is an opinion?

  E. The Komodo has large, sharp teeth.

  F. However, the Komodo dragon is still an amazing animal.

  G. Its feet have strong, sharp claws.

  H. It has a long tail and rough, scaly skin.

3. What is one reason the Komodo dragon is in danger of becoming extinct?

  A. People have destroyed some of the land where it lives.

  B. A Komodo dragon can eat very fast.

  C. It is now protected by law.

  D. Komodo dragons are only legends.

4. What is the second paragraph mostly about?

  E. What the Komodo dragon looks like

  F. How the Komodo dragon hunts

  G. What dragons are like in fairy tales

  H. What the Komodo dragon's tail looks like

▶ **Answer the questions in complete sentences.**

5. Why do you think the author wrote this article?

_____

_____

6. How does the Komodo dragon find food?

_____

_____

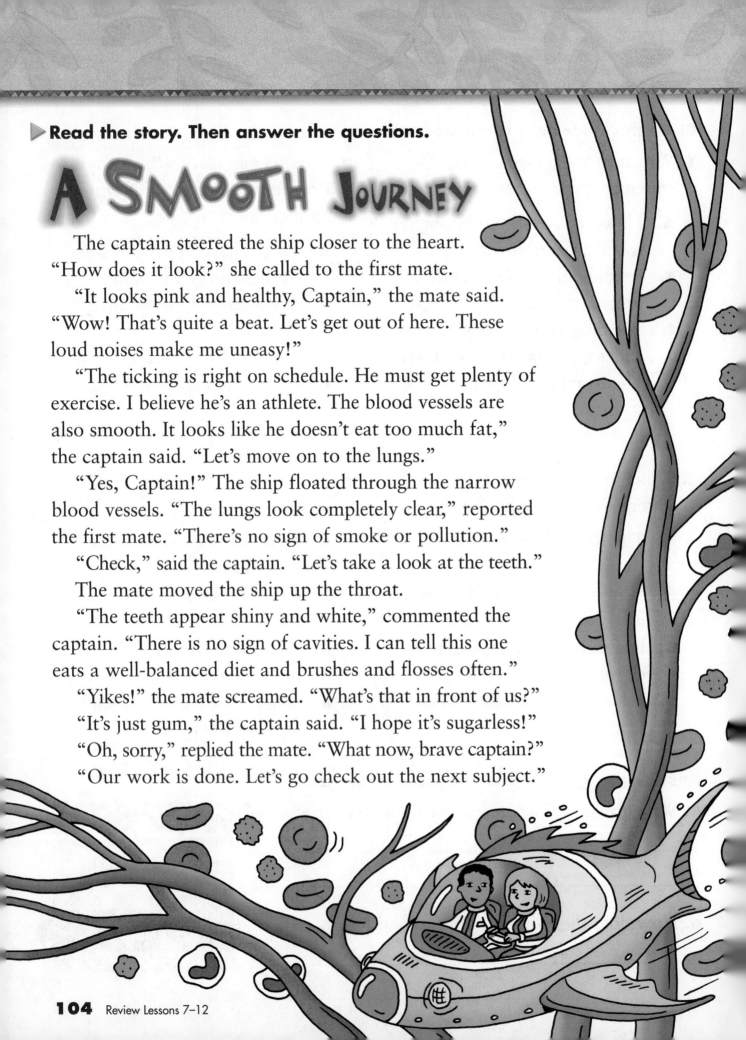

▶ **Read the story. Then answer the questions.**

A SMOOTH JOURNEY

The captain steered the ship closer to the heart. "How does it look?" she called to the first mate.

"It looks pink and healthy, Captain," the mate said. "Wow! That's quite a beat. Let's get out of here. These loud noises make me uneasy!"

"The ticking is right on schedule. He must get plenty of exercise. I believe he's an athlete. The blood vessels are also smooth. It looks like he doesn't eat too much fat," the captain said. "Let's move on to the lungs."

"Yes, Captain!" The ship floated through the narrow blood vessels. "The lungs look completely clear," reported the first mate. "There's no sign of smoke or pollution."

"Check," said the captain. "Let's take a look at the teeth." The mate moved the ship up the throat.

"The teeth appear shiny and white," commented the captain. "There is no sign of cavities. I can tell this one eats a well-balanced diet and brushes and flosses often."

"Yikes!" the mate screamed. "What's that in front of us?"

"It's just gum," the captain said. "I hope it's sugarless!"

"Oh, sorry," replied the mate. "What now, brave captain?"

"Our work is done. Let's go check out the next subject."

Fill in the circle next to the best answer.

1. According to the story, what helps to keep the heart healthy?

   Ⓐ Chewing gum

   Ⓑ Regular brushing and flossing of teeth

   Ⓒ Plenty of exercise

   Ⓓ Living where the air is clean

2. This story takes place—

   Ⓔ inside a house

   Ⓕ inside a lazy body

   Ⓖ inside an unhealthy body

   Ⓗ inside a healthy body

3. Which of the following best describes the first mate?

   Ⓐ Calm

   Ⓑ Nervous

   Ⓒ Tired

   Ⓓ Brave

4. What was most likely the author's purpose for writing this story?

   Ⓔ To entertain readers

   Ⓕ To make readers worry

   Ⓖ To teach doctors how to give checkups

   Ⓗ To tell what happens on a ship

Answer the questions in complete sentences.

5. How would you describe the body in this story?

_____

_____

_____

6. How might the story be different if it took place inside a different body?

_____

_____

_____

Glossary

algae (AL jee) Small plants that grow in water **page 3**

bison (BY suhn) A large wild animal sometimes called a buffalo **page 94**

camouflage (CAM uh flazh) Coloring or body parts that help an animal look like its surroundings **page 35**

canopy (KAN uh pee) A covering or top layer **page 55**

career (kuh REER) The work or jobs that a person does in his or her life **page 70**

celebration (sel uh BRAY shuhn) A special event or day **page 26**

colonies (KOL uh neez) Groups that live together **page 2**

comeback (KUM bak) To return **page 94**

communication (kuh MYOO ni kay shuhn) Sharing information and ideas by talking or writing **page 79**

competed (kuhm PEET id) Took part in a contest **page 71**

confidence (KON fuh duhns) A belief in yourself and your abilities **page 73**

council (KOWN suhl) A group that makes decisions **page 26**

crest (KREST) Part of an animal's body that rises above its head **page 36**

cruel (KROO uhl) Mean **page 10**

dense (DENS) Very thick **page 55**

design (di ZYN) To plan how something will look **page 21**

destruction (di STRUK shuhn) The act of ruining something **page 56**

detectives (dee TEK tivz) People who find information and solve crimes **page 43**

device (di VYSSE) A machine that does a certain job **page 80**

disable (dis AY buhl) To take away the ability to do something **page 88**

downpour (DOUN por) A very
heavy rain **page 65**

ecosystem (EE koh siss tuhm) A group
of plants and animals that need
each other to live **page 2**

endanger (in DAYN juhr) To cause
danger **page 5**

equator (ee KWAY tuhr) The imaginary
line around the center of Earth
page 54

exhausted (eg ZAWS tud) Very tired
page 28

extinct (ex TINKT) No longer living
page 56

fearful (FIHR fuhl) Afraid **page 45**

features (FEE chuhrz) Parts of an
animal's or person's body **page 21**

fiesta (fee ES tuh) A kind of party
page 18

fragile (FRAJ uhl) Easy to break
page 11

fringe (FRINJ) A row of thin pieces of
fabric or paper that hang down
page 21

frisky (FRIS kee) Playful and
full of energy **page 42**

grasp (GRASP) To take hold of **page 37**

gravity (GRAV uh tee) The force that
pulls things down and keeps them
from floating into space **page 87**

harmless (HARM liss) Not able to
cause damage **page 44**

herds (HURDZ) Large groups of
animals **page 95**

highlight (HY lyt) The best part
of something **page 73**

homestead (HOHM sted) A piece of
land belonging to settlers **page 64**

hopeless (HOHP liss) Feeling like the
worst will happen **page 43**

imitate (IM uh tayt) To copy someone
or something **page 70**

slingshot (SLING shot) A tool for hitting a target **page 62**

slither (SLITH uhr) To slide along **page 63**

species (SPEE sheez) Groups of living things that have some of the same features **page 55**

stampede (stam PEED) People or animals making a sudden, wild rush in one direction **page 64**

streamers (STREEM uhrz) Long, thin paper strips **page 21**

successful (suk SES fuhl) Doing well **page 45**

supported (suh PORT id) Helped and believed in someone **page 71**

sway (SWAY) To move back and forth **page 36**

technology (tek NOL uh jee) The use of science to make life easier **page 78**

tentacles (TEN tuh kuhlz) Long, thin parts of an animal's body used for moving or feeling **page 4**

tepees (TEE peez) Cone-shaped tents **page 96**

tracking (TRAK ing) Following a person or an animal **page 62**

traditional (truh DISH uh nuhl) Something that is passed down from parents to children **page 18**

transportation (TRANS pur TAY shuhn) A way of moving from place to place **page 81**

tropics (TROP iks) The very hot area near the equator, or center of Earth **page 54**

uncertain (un SUR tun) Not sure **page 89**